Song Of My Life

A Journey
to the
Feet
of
SATHYA SAI BABA

~

Jeannette Caruth

LEEL**A** INC.
PRESS
A Non-Profit Corporation
Faber, VA

First published in 1996 by
Leela Press, Inc.
4026 River Road
Faber, VA 22938
(804)361-1130

Library of Congress No. 96-076437

Song of My Life: journey to the feet of Sathya Sai Baba/
    written by Jeannette Caruth.

ISBN 0-9629835

Typeset in 12 point Marin

I Lay This Song of My Life
at the
Golden Feet
of
My Beloved Lord of Unfathomable Glory

Sri Bhagavan
Sathya Sai Baba

FOREWORD

A Spiritual Saga

Here is an inspired and inspiring poem by an ardent seeker of the divine - a humble American housewife who ended her search for God at the Feet of Bhagavan Sathya Sai Baba.

The inspiration was derived from her authentic spiritual experience in a series of pilgrimages to the abode of Bhagavan Baba at Prasanthi Nilayam.

The spiritual saga is inspiring because it relates in "profuse strains of unpremeditated art," the ecstatic experiences she had in her encounters with Bhagavan Baba.

Jeannette Caruth tells the story of her transformation in fluent poetry which occasionally rises to the heights of spiritual revelation. Her poem reminded me of three great authors: John Bunyan, author of *The Pilgrim's Progress*, S. T. Coleridge, well known for his poem *The Rime of the Ancient Mariner* and Walt Whitman's *Song of Myself.* After her sixth visit to Bhagavan she experienced a "taste of timelessness" about which she writes:

> I encountered from time to time
> - the evaporation of the limits that mark time
> - the unnecessary build-up of its frame
> - the viewing of the experience of one moment
> Unique in its manifestation
> naked in its aspect
> untouched by labels prefabricated by the mind

Such freedom arose from this blank slate -
How utterly joyful became the moment -
not perceived as a fragment in a pattern
but as a single, individual happening -
not asking to be liked or disliked -
and with this superb simplicity of being present
the Dance of Eternity captured my soul.

From that moment her entire life was transformed. Baba became the central force in her life. Songs in His praise came spontaneously. And then, this *Song of My Life* - a fitting testimony to the glorious fulfillment she found at the end of her journey to the Feet of Baba.

No one can go through this poetic Saga without feeling the thrill of a journey to God in the company of a devotee immersed in Divine Bliss.

V. K. Narasimhan
Editor, *Sanathana Sarathi*

V.K Narasimhan was a journalist for 50 years connected with *The Hindu of Madras, the Indian Express, the Financial Express* and the *Deccan Herald* of Bangalore. He was the first recipient of the Bhagavan Das Goenka Foundation Award for excellence in journalism. This award, instituted in 1983, corresponds to the Pulitzer Prize. He is also the author of three biographies of Indian national leaders and a historic book on the Indian Emergency of 1975-77.

CONTENTS

Dedication

Foreword

Contents

Preface

The Beginning 1

The Preparation 5

My School 10

And the Learning Continues 14

First Visit 22

Second Visit 29

Third Visit 35

Fourth Visit 48

Fifth Visit 54

Sixth Visit 65

Seventh Visit 74

Eighth Visit 85

Ninth Visit 100

And the Song Continues 112

Epilogue 117

Glossary 118

PREFACE

Unable to leave my pen idle for a long time,
I felt very prompted to write to a dear friend of mine
my recollections of the times during which
I most clearly could see the Divine Touch
of our Lord's Hand.
Such elation I experienced by doing so and
sweet joy my friend felt as she read
these accounts of Love and Light ...
It is my wish to share with you this joy,
       this elation, the happiness of this Song ...

           JC.

THE BEGINNING

Of no interest is my life as a human being
but as a child of God my life is a song ...

Out of sheer love for His Glory
I wish to tell you about
the Glory of His Love ...
I would like to relate to you, my dear friend,
the story of His Song.
What else is worth dwelling upon than
the utter Sweetness of His infinite, meticulous Care ...

Young I was ~ when oftentimes ~
sudden spells of happiness kept me spellbound.
The blue skies, with the occasional drifting by of clouds,
would summon me to partake of their depthless depth,
and perfect peace wrapped itself around my young soul ~
inexplicable joy would surge through my being.
Those were the early whispers of the
silent communications with my Lord.
Reminders of my Heavenly Home ...
and promises of the exalted joys
this life had in store for me.
In my longing to find expression
I urged this body to dance ~ unhindered I would lose myself
to the melody of the Classics
and effortlessly I revelled in His Joy.
I stumbled through the uncertain grounds of youth

and soon young adulthood brought me
face to face with my own finity.
I was diagnosed with a fatal disease ~
and death was supposed to arrive
within approximately three months.
Darkness robbed the lustre of my heart,
fright gripped my bewildered mind.
Gradually His Grace made light the seemingly heavy load ~
as He told me softly about His Glorious Land
which I was soon to enter ...
Swiftly the anxieties of a future life,
with its endless possibilities,
drifted away from me and serenity took possession of my mind
and my heart rejoiced.
Colors became of a deeper color,
music exposed its higher melody
and the Sun almost bent down to kiss my happy cheeks.
Relatives were mourning my fate ..
while joyful anticipation became my dwelling place.
With great suddenness ~ the doctors reversed the prognosis
and no longer was death expected.
The family rejoiced ...
and in the midst of their celebration
I sank to a level of great sadness and utter loneliness ...
My future life I had erased ~
no longer did I welcome the thought
of binding shackles of a possible marriage,
the trials of motherhood,
the harshness of an insensitive world.

2

I did not want to participate
in the masquerade of the blind ...
Reluctantly I resumed daily life,
.. but, the fear for lack of sufficient courage
had opened wide the gaping cry of helplessness.
The wonderful fertile soil for surrender emerged ...
A deep longing for one who could take me
by the hand and lead me safely
through the wilderness of life was born.
And quickly the irreversible response came ...
O how fortunate I was ..
The Lord sent me a Messenger Divine
a Knower of Light
a Master of Life.
In the center of a bustling European city
I was granted seven conversations
with my noble Friend, before he left his earthly sojourn.
Glorious were the moments of our togetherness,
always on Thursdays ...
Often we would abide in total Silence,
seated by his fireplace.
Penetrating looks from underneath his heavy eyebrows
would lift me to unspeakable heights.
In blissful rapture he prepared
my soul for an ever deepening search.
He imbued in me the relentless courage
to traverse the Stage of Life...
He made more complete my hesitant vision of
my somewhat hazy eyes,

thus far glanced to find a Spark of Light
but now transformed into the one-pointed
search for the Fire Divine ..
He guided my longing into a binding link
between my Lord and me ...
and so ...
for the first time I became consciously aware
of the Divine Call and the assured certainty
of its fulfillment, of which this yearning was
but the first announcement of its desired manifestation.
Barely touching the ground
of the streets in Amsterdam ~
I would somehow, after these heavenly visits,
make my way home into the country.
Before he left his human body ~
he spoke with great love about my future,
knowing my anxiety and distress about
his impending departure.
Reassuringly he told me that I would not be left alone
during this earthly journey,
on my eager quest for a divinely inspired life.
Out of my connection with him
a wonderful Love would come about, so he told me ...
Somewhat consoled I kept his words within my heart
and wondered ...
where ...
when ...
and who ...?

THE PREPARATION

Soon my wings needed a wider span
and this fledgling sought the vastness of America.
The majestic shores of the Pacific Ocean
made soar my wanderlust soul ...
It held captive the restlessness of the mind,
for it seemed to utter promises of Gold ...

For a short period of time
I lost myself in a worldly way of living.
Not until much later did I understand
why this veil had to temporarily blur my vision.
It was all part of His Plot ...
His Love, unnoticed, paved the way
for a thorough cleansing..

In the midst of my indulging in earthly activities
I suddenly felt called to enjoy
a quiet evening with the members of the Theosophical Society.
The lady spoke of her recent visit to India
where she bathed in the Presence of Sathya Sai Baba.
Slides showed the surroundings of this remote place
with loving reflections of His Form.
Deeply impressed by her genuine sincerity
and her aura of revered silence,

I decided to hold on to her name.
But as of yet, I was not ready ...
It was the planting of the seed.
It was the sweet announcement of His Arrival..
Even though my ears did not hear ~
my heart kept in hiding this great secret.

In vague surroundings,
a sharp contrast with my lofty ideals,
I was to meet the one
who would become my companion for life.
Often veiled by a curtain of alcohol
and bereft of financial security,
he seemed such an unlikely partner.
Nonetheless I felt a great pull towards this man.
An inner voice urged me to step aside
the so-called logical promptings and
habitual conclusions of the frightened mind
and instead persuaded me to follow my heart
and in bewilderment I obeyed ...
Soon I found that I truly loved this man ~
oftentimes, very unexpectedly he would display
an astounding knowledge of Truth,
but in my spiritual immaturity I did not recognize
where he came from ...

As for now I was to be blinded
by the heavy circumstances he brought about.
In order for me not to avoid these unfamiliar difficulties

'fate' decided that motherhood would keep me rooted
and face the inescapable challenge ...
Firmly pressed on all sides I suddenly remembered
the experience of the peaceful haven, which I had felt
two years ago, while listening to the radiant lady
speak about the Wondrous Holy Man, Sri Sathya Sai Baba..
The continuous confusion of my new life-style
made me hasten to this lady.
Carrying my baby girl in my arms
I timidly knocked on her door.
Quite taken aback I was
when I entered her living room
which was turned into an elaborate shrine-room.
But soon my keenness to learn about
the source of her peace
made me forget the unusual decor
and for three hours I drank in the amazing stories,
she so graciously related to me.
about the Greatness of this Holy Man.
The transformation she had undergone
struck a chord in my heart
and I knew that I had to delve deeper
into the Mystery which had presented
itself to my anxious mind.

Lo and behold ...
that very same night Sai Baba appeared in my dream.
The foremost question in my mind,
I uttered to Him:

"Is this marriage the correct one for me?"
Without hesitation His reply came,
the tone firm and unquestionable,
"Without a doubt! I give you My Blessings!"
So very reassuring was His answer
that at first I was elated and peace soothed my being.
Soon afterwards fear and bewilderment
became uppermost in my mind.
If all this was correct
how was I to cope with the intense insensibilities
of alcohol-related behavior?
How was I to live a spiritual life with one
who seemed to be opposed to higher ideals,
was reckless about money-matters,
and for whom the word future with the 'quest for stability'
had no meaning?
If Sai Baba took the time
to come and answer my question ...,
how does He expect me to live
a 'proper' life in maddening surroundings?
Many were my questions
and despair gripped my baffled mind.
In order to discover more about this new found Teacher
I made frequent visits to a sweet friend of the lady
who happened to live much closer by.
Blinded by shackles of fear
I did not want to be ridiculed by my husband
and I went under the pretense of taking sewing lessons!
My 'sewing lessons' were delightful sessions

during which slowly but surely
the magnitude of the Greatness of Sathya Sai Baba
was revealed to me.
Sparkles of joy would rise up
out of my withered soul, caused by
the realization of the unbelievable fact
that the Lord had taken human form.
The value of my human birth
during the auspicious Advent of the Avatar
started to dawn on me ...
I was hooked ...
He had fastened the cord.
And now after He had created
the proper 'props' for the set,
prepared my stage for His Plot
and made certain that I remained put ...,
He deemed the time right for me
to commence His Journey of Faith.

MY SCHOOL

My 'training ground' was soon expanded
with the arrival of a baby-boy.
Now the picture was more complete:
my ties with Mother Earth more solid,
the possibilities for worries and anxieties more vivid ...
In these irreversible surroundings
the Lord made squirm my staggering mind
but He did not abandon me ...
As soon as I had reached the conclusion
that He was the one and only God ...
He whisked me away from any contact with fellow-devotees.
My sweet 'sewing lessons' had to come to an end,
since the restlessness of my husband
made us move through different states of America.
never lingering long at one place ...,
never knowing where money or shelter
would come from ...
In order not to extinguish fully
the dimly flickering Light in my heart
I had no choice but to let go,
to the best of my ability, these mundane worries,
no matter how unwelcome these facts were,
made ever so harsh on account
of the two beautiful babies.
The awareness of the pettiness of conventionality
would gradually make its way through
my rusty, old-fashioned thinking ...
At regular intervals,

when hardships almost seemed unbearable ~
the Lord would steadfastly arrive
in my dream during many a blessed night ..!
Thoroughly soothing my soul!
He made His Appearance with such glowing Love,
that I would instantly forget
that one could experience pain on this mortal plane ...
O ~ how He suffused me with renewed courage ...
How He bound me with the unbreakable cord of Love ...
Never ~ never would I want to lose
sight of Him ...
"O ~ how can I capture Thee,
Lord of my heart, please tell me ...?"
Such were my thoughts of elation
after these Divine Visitations.
My outer difficulties would not lighten up
but He coaxed me more and more
to step back and watch ~
but NOT to run away...!
Face the humiliations which society lashes out on you,
when clothed by seemingly 'improper environments'
for a family of four.
Go beyond their ideas ...
Forego their judgements ...
Dive deep into calm waters
where their disdain cannot reach you...
Soon He began to give detailed advice
during these 'nocturnal interviews' ~
what my reaction was to be
towards intoxicated behavior,

how to decipher between the real husband
and the one who seemed to mock all sanity ...
What to say and when not to say ...
How much lighter He made my burden ..!
The certainty of not being alone
lifted the crippling load from my shoulders.
Such wondrous discoveries He brought me ...
At times my circumstances were almost transparent
and I could boldly laugh at
what the world would call a 'tough life'.

Finally after a few years of uncertainty of locations,
the coastal part of Southern California
seemed agreeable to us.
Never will I forget the day,
when after traveling through many places,
we, once again, came upon the shores of the west coast.
Suddenly I was engulfed by a wave of Bliss.
In the midst of desperate uncertainties:
with a borrowed car, borrowed money, no furniture,
two children in diapers and no particular destination in view,
I found myself raised to such a state of exultation ..!
With tears of joy, I marvelled at
this sudden Divine outpour ...,
.. and softly His Voice came:
*"It is here where you will find a great part
of your higher aspirations fulfilled".*
Overjoyed I was ~ when at the next stop
my husband found a job and we settled down
close to the roaring waves of the Pacific.

Soon ~ my longing heart cried out
for the company of fellow-devotees.
Not long afterwards I stumbled upon a person
reading a book adorned with the picture of my Beloved Lord ...
O ~ how it took my breath away ...
This confrontation led me to a lovely group
of young 'Sai' mothers, struggling with finding
the harmony between their family duties and
their aspirations for a higher life.
Such consolation I found in our group-meetings ...
Now .. at regular set times
I had the assurance of fellowship
Now ... every week
I could escape in the supreme delight
of listening to soul-stirring bhajans
Now ... I had the certainty of knowing
that, at least once a week, I could meditate undisturbed
in the peaceful, sacred environment
of a carefully decorated Altar ...!

Yes ~ He was tightening the knot ...
the pattern of worship became more concrete
and more frequent became my sweet communications,
more intense my longing for His Presence ...
and with all this 'settling' in His Beauty
the 'settling' of outer problems became
more solidified as well ......

AND THE LEARNING CONTINUES ...

With the arrival of a more or less regular life-style,
the tendency to indulge in alcohol
manifested itself in an equally regular pattern ~
with a steady sinking into further depths,
due to its attraction to a spiral motion.
The vicious cycle became solid
and the very frequent late-night struggles
with their all too familiar territory,
shortened my sleeping hours considerably.
Two bright-eyed toddlers would force me to arise
and face yet another day ...
Although the common trials of motherhood
would bring me physical fatigue,
I never felt the emotional burden of having
to raise and mould 'personalities.'
My sweet Lord had softened my hardships
by sending me two beautiful souls.
From the very beginning I sensed
that these beings were far from 'new' to this world
and very well acquainted with the Lord's Land of Light.
On many an occasion their expressions
justified these thoughts.
One such instance comes to mind ...
When my daughter, at the time 5 years old,
taught me the following lesson.
As we were busily working on a school project,
I expressed my feelings of fatigue
and my desire to rest.

14

Immediately she responded:
"Well ~ rest in your mind!
Imagine yourself lying down on the bed.
Concentrate on how your body would feel,
put that feeling in your mind and keep it there.
That is resting in the mind!"
Quite surprised, I inquired if she does this herself.
"O, yes, all the time," she replied without hesitation.
Much rest I did not get ~ but plenty of teachings!
How precious the memory of my then 4 year old son ~
who posed an interesting question to me.
Putting his hand on his heart, he said,
"What is this? What do I feel?"
I thought he meant the heart ~
but that was incorrect.
"The heartbeat?" I wondered.
"No, no", he said impatiently.
"It is God! He is inside my heart knocking constantly,
reminding me all the time: "I am HERE ~ I am HERE!
So whenever I want, I can feel Him,
I just put my hand on my heart!"
Moments like these would keep me
from drowning in worldly dross and
would heighten my longing for
an ever deeper contact with the Truth.

Maddening became my yearning
to see the Lord in the Concrete Form.
I deemed this an utter impossibility
which caused the agony of separation

15

to be ever more severe ...
At times I felt like thrusting my head
against the wall ...
instead it would droop down on my table
and profuse tears would swell my eyes.
Convinced I was ~ that I had to wait for another life-time,
maybe at the Feet of Prema Sai ...
But to no degree did this misty thought console me.
Meanwhile my Lord would try to give me hope
by telling me, many times in dreams,
that I would come to Him ...
Too aware of my inability
to grasp His perception of Time and Space,
I simply thought that the realization of this promise
was to take form at a very distant place and time.
Somewhere ... sometime ... in His Scope of Infinity.

Suddenly He started to point out,
in no uncertain terms, that it was time
to let Him "out of the closet",
where thus far I had ~ indeed ~
kept hidden all my books and pictures.
I had found the uneasiness
of a possible negative attitude from my husband
towards my Beloved Lord, too hard to bear.
.. But, now ~ no escape was offered,
He persuaded me strongly to disclose
my Sacred Secret to my life's partner ...

Anxiety would fill my mind
when pondering over the upcoming confrontation,
and many words I played over and over again
in my mind as a preparation for this unveiling.
One early morning,
I had gathered the needed courage ...
and as gently as possible
I started to tell him about the existence
of a most extraordinary Holy Man in India.
His silence encouraged me to tell more ...
Finally I stopped and waited
breathlessly for his response ...
O ~ what sweet surprise his words brought me,
"If He ever comes to America, I would like to go to Him."
The first step was taken and full of joy
I wished to relate to him the wondrous miracles He performs.
Instantly He stopped me and
said with great insistence in his voice,
"I do not need to hear about miracles.
I am His greatest miracle!" ..
His words sank deep into my being.
There was suddenly a sacred silence around us
and somehow I knew, that one day
I would find out much more about this man
who, most of the time, would so diligently hide himself ~
but yet ~ could declare statements of profound Truth ...
He broke the silence by informing me
that he had known all along that I was hiding books
and that my 'sewing lessons' had little to do with sewing,
since as of yet I could not sew a stitch ...!!

Quietly amused by my silliness
he had decided to keep silent and patiently
wait until I had reached a higher degree of maturity.
Meanwhile I had played a hide-and-go seek game
with an image of my own mind.
This I had created out of fear
of being ridiculed by my husband ~
but now, I was ridiculed by 'myself' ...

For the first few weeks afterwards
my expectations soared high ...
He seemed to have an open mind
and even started to read books
about the Glory of this Holy Man ...
My imagination ran wild and in my eager haste
I thought our troubles to be over ...
.. But, now ~ my Lord became stricter with me
and no longer accepted any behavior on my part
that would be conducive to his drinking.
No longer was I to cover up
any of the consequences he had brought
upon himself by excessive indulgence ...
I was to take a firm stand ~
instantly my husband closed the books.
His initial openness turned into a most negative attitude ...
.. and so, the extreme uneasiness
of having a partner who belittled what I treasured most,
now became a very painful reality ...
Suddenly, I no longer was looked upon
by him as an 'angel from heaven,'

but I had become a 'servant of the devil' ...
Shattered was the pedestal he had put me on.
I truly could find no other succor
than from the One, Whom I had obeyed ..
"O ~ what now, my Lord ...
where do I go ...
where are You leading me ...?"

Again He came in dreams
with the same promise, soon I would come to Him.
By now, my anxiety about reaching His Feet ~
had sharpened my awareness during my dream-state,
and quickly I asked,
"O, Lord do you mean in 'my time' or 'Your Time'...?
Amused by my question, He smiled and answered:
"Your time! I am Rama ~ you are Sita!
I am coming to take you Home.
We have played for many aeons ~
but now ... your time is up . ..."!
Supremely overjoyed, I awoke.
And for the first time, I knew that
somehow, I was to behold my Lord soon ...
So much strength I derived from His Message,
that I felt ~ I could lift mountains ...
And yes ... there was yet another mountain
to be climbed before I was allowed
to undertake the Holiest of all Holy Pilgrimages...

On one clear summer day,
I felt stopped in my movements,

as I was walking in my garden ~
a veil was taken from my eyes
and I was unmistakably told
.. that I had to leave my husband
in order to be able to come to
the Concrete Presence of the Divine,
and that this would be the only way
by which my husband would turn towards the Lord ...
Immediately the clarity of these words became clouded
by the fear of the heartbreaking execution of this command .

O ~ how could I leave this man
to whom I was deeply attached ...
whom I loved so much, inspite of all . ..
with whom I had such a strong bond ...?
Somehow ... somewhere ... hadn't there always been
an indescribable connection ...?
In great despair I tried to prepare
for this most unexpected turn...
The moment came when I informed him about my decision.
Thoroughly agonizing were the times
when I watched as the pain struck his heart
and how in total disbelief he took
this most unwelcome announcement.
In blind faith I carried out this severe command ...
Listlessness filled my lonely days,
.. only the Lord's Promise gave me life to breathe ...

Not long did I have to wait.
After a few weeks of separation,

after the initial anger had subsided,
my husband had reached a point,
where he began to inquire with great intensity
into my reasons for breaking up.
From the depth of my heart
I shared with him my desire to find
in the partner of my life a genuine longing to find God ...
I did not ask that this seeking should follow
the same path to which I was drawn...
that all I wished for was an awareness of the Divine Absence
and the consequent aching to fill this Void ...
and, that ... if one would approach with simple open-
mindedness the teachings of Sai Baba ...
one would not leave empty-handed.
Somehow this logic made sense to him ...
It was soon after this conversation
that he informed me, that suddenly he had received
an unexpected sum of money from an overdue will
from his aunt who had died many years ago!
It turned out to be just enough for some
outstanding bills and two tickets to India.
He offered to accompany me to this Holy Land ...
so he could explore the teachings of this Great Soul
and I could find fulfillment of my dearest wish ...

FIRST VISIT

Ten years had passed since I had first learned
of the Presence of the Avatar on Earth
and now finally the 'impossible' was made possible ~
I was on my way to behold my Lord ...

Thoroughly exhausted we arrived,
but my fatigue was not overwhelming enough
to keep me from my first afternoon Darshan.
My husband was overcome with sleep
and quite unaware of his 'strange' surroundings,
when I fumbled through putting on my first sari
in preparation for this most auspicious moment ...
Dazed by the uneasiness of the long journey,
I, somehow, made my way through the ashram
and found the gathering of ladies, neatly lined up.
My heart was bursting with excitement ...
as we silently seated ourselves
in front of His Glorious Temple.
I was wondering if any one could notice
the exalted state of my mind ...
It was hard to remain quiet ~
I so much wished to share my joy
with my fellow-pilgrims and tell them that
this was 'my moment' for which I had waited
and suffered for ~ for so long ..!
I controlled myself and waited for Him ...
Then suddenly He appeared ...
In silent jubilation I exclaimed,

"O Lord ~ I finally made it! I am actually here!"
I watched Him talk to the college boys
before making His way over to the ladies' side.
It was all so familiar.
My dreams had been so vivid ... so accurate ...
Quietly He passed me by ...
My eyes were riveted upon His Form.
His Sight ~ so soothing to my mind ...
Perfectly content, those first few days,
I drank in the Grace of those Precious Moments ...

.. until the wandering mind began to wonder!
Caught in the fear of its time-framed web
it sought desperate answers.
My husband I had brought ...
what now, my Lord ...?
where do You wish me to go from here ...?
My rush for relief threatened to freeze my receptive heart.
Confused I was ...
since our dream-conversations had been so clear,
so direct ..., and now I had to watch
as He would go by without a glance,
without the spoken words He had so lovingly and
generously showered me with over so many years!!
Thus ~ He gradually changed His Mode of Teaching.
I did not yet understand and
I was a somewhat unwilling student ...
not yet comfortable in His new classroom.
I felt as if purposely He would cloud my mind ...
leave me baffled by unwelcome worries,

unnecessary thoughts and sad about
my lack of elation, while in the Presence of the Divine ~
so He could work undisturbed on my heart and soul.
As if He were protecting my dull-witted mind
from an overdose of Light ...,
Which He poured into my being,
but Which was not to surface so instantly, so abruptly ~
but was to suffuse my soul gently and gradually,
as time would tell and unfold ...
Not aware of these subtleties at that moment,
I would sometimes feel abandoned ...
His Compassion, however, did not allow me
to reach a very dry depth.
He wished to console this little child ...,
so new to His mysterious Ways.

One beautiful afternoon, I was awaiting His Arrival
with a camera on my lap, anxious to immortalize
these unique moments of my proximity to the Avatar ...
as I was thoroughly uncertain if
He would ever allow me to return ...!
From afar I watched Him come nearer and nearer.
When He had almost reached the place
where I was seated, I quickly clicked my camera ...
Immediately afterwards ~
He pierced His Eyes into mine ...
nothing remained at that moment.
Shocked to the core was my being
by this sudden confrontation with the Divine Absolute!
He whisked away my soul .

I lost my imagined possessions ~
and in that brief instant
nothing mattered ... nothing existed ...
The minute He let go of my eyes
tears started to flow, I was incapable of thinking ...
unable to do anything ...
I allowed my being to be overwhelmed
by this outpour of Grace ...
Gently the words of prediction by my first Teacher,
came back to my mind.
How blissfully he had mused over my future!
.. And now, I understood why!!

Within a few days the answer to my main question came,
I had to stay with my husband ...
This was my path ..
and as always, He would help me ...
Meanwhile my husband had adjusted quite well
to the unfamiliar environment of the ashram.
Through observing, reading and listening
he started to accept more and more
these fundamental teachings.
At the end of our stay he confessed that
somehow all his questions had been answered.
Quite content he seemed that he had been able
to undergo this spiritual adventure
without any inner discomfort.
He was satisfied with his findings and
now was ready to return to the Western World.
I sensed that there was not a great intensity

behind these revelations that might have caused
him to alter his ways drastically ...
but for now I was to be content
that the seed was planted and that he had accepted
my interest in spiritual endeavors.

Once back home ~ life seemed to continue
along, more or less, the same route.
Our finances however started to diminish.
By now my husband had built his own business
and suddenly this began to crumble.
Frightened about a repetition of those struggling years,
I became very unsure if I could survive
such strenuous living without
the assured certainty of seeing my Lord.
Even though He had so thoroughly sustained
my being with His Love and His Grace ~
now ... I could not abandon the desire
to bathe again and again in His Ocean of Mercy ...
I cried out for help to Him and quickly His solution came.
A lovely family of devotees had just bought
a beautiful, large home.
He urged me to offer to clean
this home once a week in exchange
for an annual plane-ticket to India ..!
In this way ~ no money would be brought into the household
with the added temptation for improper use.
And so it happened ...
elated I was ~ when they accepted this suggestion.
No longer did I have to wonder

when and how ...
Now my days were so much brighter
for I could count them in joyful anticipation
for the ever-longed for Darshan of the Divine ...!
The impact of this first visit had a very gradual effect.
I could feel that the sharp edges of worldly living
were no longer so pronounced.
Much more soothed I was and
often I would find myself in wordless conversation with Him ...
Nothing was really the same ~
yet outwardly ~ it all seemed unchanged.
Ever beckoning me to seek His Presence
in the solitude of my heart ...
He now forbade me to participate any longer
in discussion groups.
Ever encouraging me to rely only
upon my own ear to hear His Promptings,
He wished for me not to divert my attention,
to scatter my insights or fall prey to
the 'game of comparison' ~ so often found
in the early stages of 'seeking'!
He allowed me to sit and listen
to the heavenly bhajans.
Always ~ this cleared the way instantly ...
and my jubilant heart would find itself at His Footstool ...
my soul quickly enraptured by the Flow of Divine Energy.
Effortlessly it would raise my whole being
into His timeless Melody ...
There I would find the nourishment
needed to carry me through the worldly duties,

to brace me against uncommon hardships,
to reassure me again and again
of His constant inner Guidance ...

A sweet surprise awaited me
when I had my pictures developed ...
Anxious to have a visual remembrance,
I hurriedly looked for the one,
taken just before that momentous moment
of His graceful Look.
Instead ...I found one picture as if taken
just after that glorious instant.
I tried to recapture these moments
over and over again in my mind ...
and always came upon the same conclusion.
It was impossible for me to have taken
a picture at that time,
since He had rendered me incapable
of any action or thought ...
I had been benumbed ...
I looked in wonder at this photo.
It was a close-up picture of Him
walking away from me, showing His Back.
His Message came in a flash:
"FROM NOW ON ~ DO NOT LOOK BACK
 FOLLOW ME ..."

SECOND VISIT

Soon the plan for the next trip emerged.
My brother, by now a fellow-devotee,
wished to provide the tickets for my husband and children.
At their young age, ten and eight,
they were called to bathe in His Presence.
Such fortunate souls ...!

A lovely welcome was prepared for me ...
As the family was overcome by travel-fatigue
and tried to rest up in their hotel in Bangalore ~
I took, that afternoon, a taxi to Brindavan.
Great was my surprise when I found out
that those who had just arrived or were about to depart, ...
would be ushered into the Lord's Lotus Home
for bhajans with the college boys.
My mind became stilled
by the thrill of this unexpected gift ...
One moment I had been so busily engaged
in the noises of the Western World and now ...
I was told to enter the Lord's Home!
Although I was seated in a far corner
of His small round hall, from where
I was unable to catch a glimpse of Him,
I felt so immensely grateful for having been called
once again, to His Lotus Feet ...
Fully content I drank in deep
the auspiciousness of my surroundings

and the sacredness of the Divine Songs,
.. then, suddenly He entered the Hall.
So unexpectedly had He made His entrance,
it took my breath away ...
He was like a bright Flame
thoroughly igniting my Light-seeking heart.
He passed through the hall, went upstairs
and graced us with a glance from over the balustrade.
I was called Home!!
"This, My dear child, is your Home ~
  Yes, you belong here!
  Always My door is open ...
  Do not be so surprised.
  Accept it ~ claim it.
  You are Mine ...!"
These statements sang jubilantly through my veins,
seeking a permanent abode in my heart, mind and soul.
Overwhelmed by His Grace ~
I returned to my hotel ...

Within a few days we left for Puttaparthi
where we settled in to undergo
the Divine Treatment for the next several weeks.
Again ... I was to be there,
to listen to His silent Promptings ...
to be still ...
It urged me to find a new sense of surrender ~
to allow the change from 'direct communication' in dreams
to the 'indirect attention' from His Concrete Form

to take place ...
To exercise the practice of no expectations ...
to be content with the Aura of Divinity ...
to let It heal the hasty mind ...
and encourage the timid blossoming of the heart ...
to watch the 'selfish one' become
embraced by the Selfless One ...
Sweet patience was my lesson ~
Divine Contentment ... the promise.

Unaware of our immense good fortune
the celebration of the ten-day festival of Dasara
took place during our stay.
Faintly familiar with its magnificent meaning
we bathed in the flood of Divine Energy
generated by this Holy Sacrifice ~
made profoundly auspicious
by the Presence of the Lord Himself ~
the Receiver of the worship of the Sacrifice,
the Inspirer of the Sacrifice,
the Ultimate Performer of the Sacrifice ...
O blessed days ~
A richly decorated Sai Gita ...
Holy Chants by Brahmin Priests ...
The Sacred Fire flaming high ...
The daily thrill of the Lord's Voice singing ...
~ Grace unequalled ..!
The Victory Day was to start ...
having arrived a little late,

I was shoved into an aisle seat
on the outer side of the Poornachandra Hall.
Dismissing all hope of my Lord coming near,
I eagerly watched the final process of the Sacrifice
taking place on the stage.
With a basin filled with Holy Water
the Lord came down to His Flock
and showed great delight
in His Task of sprinkling His devoted ones
with these blessed drops.
Lo and behold ... He came to my aisle
and before I could hope for this blessing
I suddenly saw His smiling Face,
He raised up His brush and drenched
my face with Sacred Water.
O ~ Joy Supreme! ...
only He knew the true blessing
of this Heavenly Shower ~
I could only experience an unspeakable elation,
an inexplicable surge of happiness,
but its inconceivable meaning escaped
my meager mind...

Sweetly spoiling the children
He gave them many an encouraging smile
and wrote for each of them
His Symbol ॐ   on a small slate ...!
Their faraway God came ever closer.
Carefully imprinting His Image indelibly

on their hearts, He made solid the link
between their 'young' souls and His Divine Self,
embodied in human form.
By the time our departure took place
He seemed satisfied with the Gifts He had granted us.
Slightly dazed by the Divine Energy
He had poured into my being
I spent the next few months in a peaceful mood ...
After this 'gestation' period ~
His new lessons would surface,
He urged me to have a set time for meditation.
Now at the very early dawn
I forced myself to leave the bed
and follow a routine for prayer and meditation.
At first ~ each morning was a struggle
as I felt that it might be inconvenient
for my husband, who was so unfamiliar
with such a practice in his own home.
In this way ~ I daily, had to overcome
this mental barrier ...
take my stand ...
fight against lazy thoughts ...
and let the Light claim victory over dreary darkness.
Slowly the regular pattern of acknowledging
His Presence, His Love, His Guidance
during these early hours
became an established part of my daily life.
The presence of an altar became such a stronghold ~

a lovely place of security ...
an expression for our devotion ...
the immediate evidence of His Divine Presence.
My wish to please Him
became more and more prominent.
A prayer expressing this desire
would often find my lips, softly I would sing,
"O Lord, how can I please Thee at all times ...
 O Lord, allow me to be able to please Thee at all times ...
 O Lord, allow me the constant desire to please Thee
at all times ...
 O Lord, allow me to please Thee ..."
How wondrous was the ever growing effect
of the Miraculous Cause of His Darshan!
Ceaselessly it would infiltrate my limited thinking,
it would alter my actions,
it would gradually elevate my feelings.
The August Auspiciousness of
the most unique Blessing of His Darshan
would raise my awareness
into an ever-increasing wonderment
.. as I watched the approach
of another Journey to His Golden Lotus Feet...

THIRD VISIT

My dreams had become fewer in frequency.
Now and then He seemed delighted to surprise me
by appearing so crystal clear during the nightly hour.
Some weeks prior to my third journey ~
I found myself, during the dream state,
on the steps of His veranda,
ready to enter the sacred interview room ...
I looked around me and was amazed
to find myself among a group of strangers.
I, nonetheless, attempted to follow this group inside,
but the Lord smilingly stopped me and said,
"It will be better to wait until the plane comes down.
 You will derive greater benefit from it at that time!"
I awoke and wondered what it was that He indicated ...
did He predict an interview ...
or maybe a plane crash ...?
I pushed aside further lingering on these possibilities ~
as I was busily engaged in preparing for this trip.
This year I was to go alone ...
Stripped of any responsibilities,
abandoning all distractions,
this sudden liberty allowed me
to sharpen my focus solely on the Light Divine ...
Almost guilty I felt, when the ties of family-life
so abruptly seemed to have disappeared

as He beckoned me to embark
fearlessly upon His Land of the Unknown.
Within a couple of days
the awareness of a secular world had quickly vanished
and I felt an opening-up of new vistas.
Beautiful insights presented with simple logic.
Hesitant I was to fully claim these new understandings ~
to accept their authenticity ...
and, consequently, to change my whole outlook ...?
The seeing of His Form ...
told me again and again
that this was the Final Sight in the world of matter.
The purpose of the existence of my senses
had come to completion.
After thousands of lifetimes
the World of Shadows held no longer any reason for being.
There was nothing left to behold ...
nothing left to hear ...
nothing left to touch ...
nothing left for the mind
to register, to collect, to ruminate about ...
for the 'limited' had come into contact with the "Limitless' ...
The created one had met with the Creator ...
What other goal was left to pursue ...?
What other sense could I find for my senses ...?
If all this was so ~ where would I go from here?
Suddenly the world of myriad forms
began to fade, no longer did forms
hold any fascination for me ...

and somehow I was left empty.
And I wondered ...
"Was I supposed to abandon the old concepts
and dive ever deeper into these new revelations?"
Was I allowed to enter into a Land of Greater Subtlety ...?
Terrified of being misled or plagued
by a 'spiritual hysteria' of my Western mind ...
I pleaded again and again with my Lord
to give me His acknowledgement
about the truth of these inner discoveries
and His permission and assurance of guidance
to go onto the next phase ...
The doors of the world of matter had been closed ...
no other door had yet been opened ...
Utterly lost I felt as the days went by
and the closing of the 'old chapter' seemed to intensify.
The Lord gave me no clue ...
no look, no glance, no smile,
no sweet inner promptings!
Desperate I became ~
for no longer did I know how to live
in a world, which had ceased to exist for me.
There was nothing left to do ~
other than to pray ...
My cry for erasing the darkness and
bringing Light into my heart became a constant one.
The Holy Gayatri was my only hope ...
Thoroughly petrified I watched
my day of departure come ever nearer.

In my total despair ~
I called upon many a great Saint
to plead with my Lord on my behalf.
I reasoned within myself
that He would listen to their Call more promptly
than to my inadequate murmur ...
So, I begged Lord Buddha ...
to beseech my Lord to shower me
with the Light of True Understanding.
I invoked Lord Jesus
to plead with our Holy Father
to have mercy upon me and show me the Way.
Mentally I gathered around me
the grand Paramahamsa Ramakrishna,
Vivekananda and all saintly friends I could think of ~
and urged them to persuade
the Lord not to leave me stranded ...
That afternoon I was to leave at six o'clock.
Tearfully and with a sense of being abandoned
I reluctantly packed my bag.
Nervously I lined up for Darshan ~
trying to brace myself for yet another disappointment.
Once on the temple ground, in the first row,
I became very upset ...
knowing that He was the Only One,
Who could ever clear my doubts
and shed Light upon my hesitant heart ...
..how could He possibly send me away in this frame of mind .?
I felt dead to the world and did not know

what to do there ...
How cruel that would be ..!
Silently I screamed out to my heavenly friends
not to let this happen!
Very slowly the Lord walked towards the ladies' side.
My heart was jumping angrily,
while my mind tried one last desperate cry
for the Grace of His Light ...
and then, very matter-of-factly,
He stopped in front of me and told me to go inside ...!

Suddenly the intense anguish evaporated.
A serene calm came over me
as I walked to His Golden Temple.
Only the prayer for Light remained in my heart.
Once inside, after giving out His Vibhutti
to the small assembly of devotees,
He invited me along with my two friends
into His private interview-room.
I quickly sat down by His Chair
.. no time did He waste.
Without mercy, but full of Grace
He started to scold me severely...
His flaming Eyes only inches away from mine ...
He fired at the array of thoughts I had entertained.
He tore to pieces the insecurity I had nourished
about my spiritual discrimination.
He seemed angry about the reluctance
I had shown in accepting the wonderful revelations,

He had showered me with.
Within seconds I knew that
all I had seen and felt, was correct.
And now ... He was opening another door.
Still unfamiliar with this new Field
I sought His Constant Guidance.
No sooner had this thought emerged
than He waved His Hand from Which
dropped a pendant on a necklace.
Ignoring my outstretched hand,
He slowly untwined the chain and with great care and
full of Love He put this Divine Gift over my head.
The silence during these moments carried me
into His timeless Realm of Perfect Order.
The chain He had materialized, was so long
that the pendant, adorned with His Image,
reached my heart ...
Now ~ after closing the Chapter of Worldly Matter,
He sealed it with His Concrete Gift,
dangling on my heart ...
reminding me to enter this Sacred Chamber
to seek ever more His Presence,
His Love, His Glory, in this Sanctuary
and forego the illusion of matter.
He looked deeply into my eyes and repeated thrice,
"I am ALWAYS with you"
.. those familiar words ~
now sounded like magic ...
To emphasize this assurance of His Guidance,

He laid His Lotus Hand upon my head.
Drinking in the unfathomable Sacredness
of these momentous moments,
I remained utterly still
while He addressed the two other ladies.
Suddenly, while He was engaged in conversing with them ...
I felt His Golden Hand forcefully
upon the crown of my head
again and again...
no thoughts were present,
the Power of His Energy seemed to penetrate
my whole being as much as possible.
While still concentrating on
this Divine Flow of Energy,
He unexpectedly asked me how my husband was!
He did not wait for an answer
but told me, slowly and diligently,
"He is a good man, a very good man,
a very, very good man!
He is a good husband, a very good husband,
a wonderful husband!"
I allowed these words to sink deep
into my consciousness without questioning Him.
He proceeded by telling me
that I would bring him next year.
"He will come next year ~ he will come ..."
As He spoke these words
He leaned back, had both His Hands raised
and closed His Eyes.

He seemed to anticipate my husband's visit
with such Bliss ...
My heart was overjoyed!
As He was bringing this private time to a close
I, suddenly, realized that what I needed most
for my Journey into His Land of Greater Subtlety
was ... concentration!
As soon as this flashed upon my mind
I uttered this request to my Heavenly Father.
Instantly He turned to me
and said: " ... yes, I will give you that!",
and repeated this three times.
We got up and entered the general interview room.
After He had spent some precious moments
with the other small groups and handed all of us
packets of Vibhuthi, He led us to the door
and ushered us back into the World,
His Field of Action ...
our Ground for Learning ...
His Land of Buried Treasures ...
for us to find and discover ...
..As I stepped over the threshold,
I beheld the college boys lighting
the little oil lamps in celebration of
the Victory of Light over Darkness ...
the Holy Festival of Deepavali ...
the Festival of Lights!!
The removal of darkness from our heart
and the igniting of Light in our Sacred Chamber ..

All I had prayed for, cried about
and despaired over ...
had been granted to me a thousandfold ~
in a manner most unimaginable ...
more complete than I ever could have fathomed ...

Drenched in His Light
suffused by His Grace
permeated by His Love
.. I entered my taxi and left the ashram.
That evening, in my hotel room in Bangalore,
I stumbled through the 'usual' routines
but now the 'usual' had become difficult to find.
I literally had to sit down and
firmly ask myself what procedures
I had to follow in order to function ...
slowly it came back to me and
I remembered that before retiring
for the night one changes into nightwear,
refreshes oneself and brushes the teeth ...!
Meanwhile during the evening and night
I was surrounded by the thundering noises of fireworks ...
an ever-deepening reminder of
the momentous significance of
the Festival of Lights ~
the very day, chosen by my Lord
to carry me over the threshold from the world of density
into an awareness of Greater Light.
His Promise made in a dream many years ago,

that "the time and date for an interview were set!"
had come to fruition !!

Very gently He allowed me
to become re-acquainted with the world of forms,
but even though the forms had not changed
I no longer perceived them as before.
From time to time I joyously beheld
the transparency of concrete forms ...
their existence being nothing
but a conglomeration of 'matter',
particles of mere dust
arranged in different modes
assuming greater or lesser shapes ...
.. their only substance consisting of Light.
None of this I found in a clear visual picture
but always it came as a very defined awareness
bringing utter calm to my whole being,
a pervasion of a deeply Sacred Stillness ...
Happily surprised by these inner treasures
I walked through this world in amazement
and enjoyed this new view ...
Quickly I learned ...
that not only the world of matter
is built up in this manner,
but also that the world of thought
is of the same structure.
Particles of 'subtle' matter clinging together
imposing their so-called 'existence' on our minds,

pounding us with their relentless persistence ~
screaming to be recognized ~
demanding attention for their 'non-existent life'
in order to prolong their span of exposure.
I discovered that with such thorough examination
their elusive presence simply dissipated
and no fear could be encountered ...
It was an astounding revelation ~
far more real than any words
I had ever read or heard about this subject.
Everything became transparent.
This penetrating observation now
came upon the entity called my personality,
the perceiver of discoveries ...,
the person built up by a conglomeration of 'thoughts' ~
trains of habitual mental patterns
solidified into a seemingly non-erasable image ...
Now, too ~ this started to dissolve into 'nothingness'.
Suddenly the folly of the Game of Shadows,
with its many varied complexities,
became amusingly clear.
The stronghold of its deception
ceased to bind me blindly ...
But ~ do understand well ~ that these wondrous revelations
were not always present at
the surface of my daily awareness!
After the first few months their intensity
tapered off and their influence fell to the background.
Even though life with all

the threatening conditional aspects
of forms, thoughts and emotions
came back to the forefront ~
somehow the thick knot of ignorance was broken ...
and I was much more capable
of diving within myself to re-live
these understandings of Light
and re-nourish my soul with their expanding impact.
His Grace had allowed me to perceive
this minute speck of His Vast Fountain of Knowledge.
Its reality had dawned on my soul ~
its secret I carried in my heart ~
and now the time-consuming process
of suffusing this element of truth throughout
my consciousness had commenced ...
I came to realize:
that .. the Sight of our Lord in human form
                carries us over the World of Forms ~
that .. the sacred repetition of His Holy Name
    allows us to traverse the Land of Thoughts and
            Emotions ~
that .. the inner Vision of His Effulgent Form
    leads us to the complete annihilation
                of the awareness of the individual self ~ ...

Great joy brought the memory
of the Lord's words spoken about my husband.
Filled with loving anticipation
I simply shoved aside any unwelcome encounter

brought about by my husband's excessive drinking.
My thoughts about the happy 'tomorrows'
made me forget the present moment.
I was convinced that the Lord had called
my husband in order to cure him
from this negative habit.
I envisioned that His Embrace
would instantly heal this destructive tendency
and he would be raised
to a level of sober contentment
and share my feelings of devotion.
O ~ how I looked forward
to being a witness to this awakening!
How wonderful that my challenging days
were numbered ...
and soon I would enjoy not only
a deeper inward peace but also
the blessing of a harmonious household!
Mostly oblivious to anything else around me ...
I spent my remaining days
in this mood of expectations ...
anxiously awaiting the moment
of departure for my fourth visit.

FOURTH VISIT

I had worked very hard during those intervening months,
in order to be able to purchase plane-tickets
for the whole family.
Nine months had elapsed ...
when we boarded the plane.
I was in a joyful state of mind during this journey,
knowing that I had fulfilled His Command
to bring my husband.
When I arrived at the ashram
I felt as if it had only been yesterday since I had left.
Fully satisfied ~ I looked forward to watch
the unfolding of His Drama for the four of us.
Especially those first few days
I felt very content ~
feeling certain that this visit would bring about
the longed-for change in my outer life,
the change that would ease my circumstances;
.. that would offer me a smoother path
which would allow me to remain more fully
focussed on my Lord Divine.
Already I rejoiced over
this Gift of sweet Grace ...
Days went by ...
None of us received any outward attention.
The Lord ignored my husband completely,
never even glanced at him!
We started to reason that most likely

the 'usual' pattern for being granted
an interview would take place ~
which meant at the last minute of our stay.
Nonetheless ~ restlessness became evident ...
nervousness about what might happen
or might not happen, prevailed for all of us.
The last day arrived ...
my husband and son as well as
my daughter and I were allowed
a front row seating since we were about to depart.
By now ~ quite uncertain about the Lord's intentions ~
I awaited anxiously His Arrival.
As soon as He came out of the Temple
He walked straight towards us
and stopped right in front of me ...
He took letters from all sides,
as I repeatedly requested an interview
emphasizing that we were leaving.
My eyes were riveted upon His Face
waiting for Him to break the icy shield
He seemed to hold between us ...
Not once ~ did He look at me ...
Suddenly I noticed His most precious Lotus Feet ...
I so much wished to lay down my head
upon this Fountain of Gold ...
but ~ was too distracted by phrasing my desire
for an interview for the 'benefit' of my husband.
The moment I realized that the Feet Divine
had been in front of me all this time ...,

and I could have reached out
and touched Them ... He left!
My heart sank ...
but ~ there was still the chance
that He would address my husband.
My heartbeat increased as He approached the men.
They too received the same treatment.
Without a sign of recognition He passed them by,
ignoring my husband's plea for an interview.
Dumbfounded ... I had to watch
the panic of my mind.
Utter confusion and thorough sadness
crushed all my hopes ...
.. and then He revealed the reason
for His 'cold behavior':
*" .. for you, My dear child, there is no room
   in My Mansion, since you imagine that you love Me,
   but you do not! You desire that I bring a change in
                                       your circumstances.
      You do not come to Me ~ out of love for Me!
      You have no right to sit at My Feet...!"*
The meaning of His reproach pervaded my soul
and instantly shot forth painful arrows at my ego.
Perfectly clear became my foolishness
but my ego was not so easily assuaged ...
In revolt ~ it slashed back at my frame
and immediately I became ill.
By the time we got in the taxi,
my fever was rising steadily.

Deep down in my soul I knew that this harsh Lesson
was a most wonderful Display of Grace
and I felt honored to be worthy
of this severe and stern warning of the Mother Divine,
~ now I simply had to endure
the discomforts of the body and
the obstinate acrobatics of the mind.
Until once again ...
I would be able to find His further Instructions
in a more peaceful state of mind.

Two weeks passed before my illness subsided.
Gradually I started to face
the inner blow I was dealt.
I realized that I had wasted
the greater portion of the previous year.
I had completely smothered the Present
in my eager anticipation for an imagined Tomorrow.
I had left the Altar in my heart ...
abandoned the adoration of my Lord ...
I had stepped out of the Temple ...
and allowed myself to become distracted
by fancying better preparations for
decorating the inner Altar ~
where I had already been seated;
that Sanctuary where I had bathed
undisturbed in His Love.
I had denied His Presence and degraded myself
by pondering over temporary and secondary circumstances.

He had so masterfully guided me,
by displaying such blissful contemplation
about my husband's arrival,
into creating the solid conclusion
of an oncoming desirable change ...
He had prepared my fall ...
laying bare the intrinsic deceptive
workings of the mind.
The mind ... always exerting itself
in overshadowing the Still and Sublime Awareness
of the Light Divine by luring us into the seeking
of false comforts and eases
for its phantom structure: our ego.
Even enticing us with promises
of an intenser awareness of the Divine ...
if only we follow its prescribed plot!
Leading us ever astray ...
always towards the outward-bound senses.
Sad I felt ~ that I had let 'slip away'
the timeless Gifts He had given me ...
I had left unused the precious insights
He had granted me ... and I had allowed
the impression for lesser pain in the future
to become more prominent in my awareness.
So deep was the wound ...
that it carved a sensitive alertness.
I prayed never to fall prey again
to such obvious deceptions!
With renewed fervor

I tried to concentrate ever harder
on Him alone ~ my beloved Lord ...
Always less than adequate did I rate my efforts ~
I felt as if I constantly fell short
of His Demands and Expectations,
but nevertheless ~ I would not give up ...
I could not give up ...
for I was determined that some day
I would LOVE ONLY HIM.

FIFTH VISIT

During my many years of cleaning the house
of my fellow-devotees, I had access to their vast library.
Graciously they allowed me to read
whatever book caught my eye.
Through these readings a deep-felt awe
for the Ancient Scriptures was born within me.
The lady of the house disclosed to me
her special fondness for the Holy Bhagavata
and related to me her wonderful experiences
while reading this Sacred Work.
Noticing my keen interest, she surprised me greatly,
when, one day, she arrived at my doorstep and
presented me with a new set of this age-old Scripture.
Two beautiful volumes covering a total of 1715 pages,
called the *Srimad Bhagavata Mahapurana*.
Words could not convey my gratitude.
Now ~ every day I allowed myself
to delve into the Mystery of these ancient words
dropped from the lips of the Great Seers.
Its inspiration would engulf me
immediately whenever I partook of its nectar
in the shape of the stories of the Divine Incarnations.
It described the Golden Promise
of heightened devotion when read
in totality within seven days.
Not a single doubt had I about
the authenticity of this statement ~

I felt irreversibly drawn to this sacred undertaking.
The Call to immerse myself
in this Ocean of Love became ever louder,
and the plan to do so
in the Presence of the Lord emerged ...!
This year I would be unaccompanied by my family
and therefore this opportunity seemed most opportune.

Arriving in Brindavan, I soon found myself
enjoying the luxury of a large room by myself.
This was quite unique ~
I perceived it as a special sign of His Approval
about my intention to complete a seven-day reading
of the Holy Bhagavata.
After a few days of rest and recuperation
from the long travel hours,
I planned my week ahead.
I would rise about four o'clock in the morning
and read until breakfast.
After breakfast I would join the lines for Darshan,
the waiting time I would fill with reading.
In the midst of the glorious stories
my eyes would be allowed the unique Grace
of beholding the One, to Whom
all the descriptions pertained ...
Once out of sight,
I again would direct my eyes to the pages
and listen attentively to Its Song Divine.
Thus ~ I would remain

under the heavenly Banyan Tree until noon.
Lunch and a short nap would refresh me
sufficiently to return to the Tree
and resume reading until six o'clock,
with another chance for Darshan.
After dinner one more hour of reading
would be left in order for me to complete
the daily intake of 250 pages.
And so I did ...

Right at the onset of this Holy occupation
I was graced with a most beautiful Vision.
I was seated under the Great Tree
and bhajans had just finished,
during which our Lord was absent
due to a short visit to Bombay ~
but ... His Absence was not felt in my heart.
With my eyes closed ~
I perceived the mind-matter as a milky substance
flowing towards the senses and
getting lost in the rivers of the world ...
Then ~ suddenly the direction of the flow changed,
now the milky substance streamed
towards the chamber of my heart
where I could see His Lotus Feet ...
The love and tenderness with which
this stream caressed His Feet Divine
overwhelmed my soul and tears of ecstasy
instantly bathed my cheeks.

For a while I was allowed to dwell
in this unique inner manifestation
of unconditional devotion ...
Then ~ the whole picture became bundled up
into a small ball and was quickly shot forth
to the crown of my head.
The impact of this 'transfer' was such
that I was afraid that I would lose consciousness.
With all my might I tried to hold on ...
the intensity relaxed when His Voice told me,
"... first I want you to get used
to the Joy of Devotion in your heart,
thus you will become prepared to withstand
the Power of the Light of My Knowledge ..."
O ~ how I treasured this Vision!
Unable to leave this holy spot
I remained seated for a long time
so as to prolong its blissful effect.
The very next dawn I started my reading ...
Every time I opened this Book I seemed to become
engulfed in the Fragrance of that sublime Vision ...
hour after hour ...
day after day ...
I became immersed in its Divine Nectar.
How unmistakably clear it was
why a seven-day reading was so strongly recommended!
No distractions were possible ...
the constant company of Its Holy Glory
surrounds one who reads with concentration.

The Presence of His Divine Energy never leaves one ...
Effortlessly the weeds are pulled out ...
and the flowers eagerly open up under
the benevolent Rays of the Shining Sun ...
Darshan was grander than ever before.
More vividly did my Lord seem to display
the different aspects of His former Incarnations:
.. the frightful Power of Lord Narasimha
.. the Majesty of Lord Rama
.. the beauteous Splendor of Lord Krishna
Once again during this week I beheld a lovely vision ...
in essence similar to the former one,
but slightly different in expression.
Now the mind-matter was shaped
in the form of a swan.
The swan had wrapped itself around His Golden Feet
and caressed with its neck tenderly the Feet Divine.
Sweet, sweet joy permeated my being
as He blessed me so profusely
with the rare taste of devotion.
As my 'seven days' came closer to completion
my love for His Feet had grown a thousandfold.
With great eagerness I looked forward
to each Darshan when I could feast upon
the sight of His long stroll towards the Tree
with my eyes fixed upon
the Lotus Feet of my Lord Supreme ...
How strong the desire became to lay my head
down at this Source of all Creation!

In my fervent prayer I asked for release
from the fascination towards the outer world
and His Grace for Supreme Devotion
to His Lotus Feet within my heart.
One afternoon during bhajans
He clearly conveyed to me that
He would seal His Promise for
the fulfillment of my prayer by granting
me padnamaskar ...
The next morning I had a front row seating ~
with the note expressing my request in hand
I calmly waited for His Arrival.
This morning He appeared exceedingly tender to me.
Such peace His Radiance exuded ...
Without any jumbling thoughts crowding my mind,
I stretched out my hand,
He took the letter ...
for a brief moment He looked into my eyes
and wordlessly acknowledged my prayerful request
and silently approved my wish for padnamaskar.
For the first time in my life
I raised up on my knees and
folded my hands around His Lotus Feet
and rested my forehead upon this Fountain of molten Gold,
where all desires melt away ...
and all promises are fulfilled ...

How fruitful it had been that He had denied me
this unique privilege the year before ..!

How much stronger my yearning had become
for this most sought-after Blessing ...
How much deeper the respect had grown
since He had revealed so sublimely the symbolism
of this most reverential expression of devotion ...
He did not allow me to experience
padnamaskar as a commonplace event ...
Its sacred significance was now imprinted on my mind;
its auspiciousness made more complete
my bow of surrender.
After this timeless moment had passed
I was approached, separately, by two fellow-devotees.
Each described their elation about the beautiful sight of
the padnamaskar I had just been granted.
Through their words He emphasized for me
His Joy of receiving my feelings of Reverence and Love.
This acknowledgement elevated
the sense of sacredness I felt upon completing
the seven-day reading of the Holy Bhagavata,
.. the ancient Scripture of Which our Lord,
in the Sandeha Nivarini says, that it is the story
of the beginningless, endless Atma ~
that it explains the real secret of the Lord and His real Glory !
Indeed ~ it had opened wide
the Door to beauteous Devotion ...
It had transported me to a different level of awareness ...
and had generated a soft, sweet pain in my heart.
The Grace that had oozed from the pages
of this most Holy Book of majestic Glory

kept my soul in a raptured awe for several weeks.
Upon my return home
the blissful aftermath allowed me
to actually experience from time to time
the changing of the mind-flow towards
the outward senses into the Seat of my Heart ...
and unspeakable love would enter my being.
I came to realize that all offerings,
sweet or pungent, were equal in taste to our Lord.
Worthy or unworthy found no distinction in Him.
He relishes each morsel ...
treasures every gift ...
and in His Supreme Delight over our thoughtfulness
He embraces us with great Love
and we find ourselves suffused by His Bliss.
In this Divine Elation the sweet merging
of the Receiver and giver takes place.
Such is the Royal Path of Supreme Devotion.
One of these sublime moments occurred
when my husband came home quite inebriated.
I had just spent some exquisite time
contemplating this marvelous secret of devotion
and fully enjoying the taste of its nectar.
As he staggered through the doorway,
I felt that no matter what condition he portrayed,
this very sight when turned over to my Lord,
would simply constitute His Food Divine.
The very thought of an offering to the Lord
generated such a flood of Love through my soul ...

that I eagerly drank in this sight
and let it flow to the Lotus Feet of my Lord
within my heart ...
Exaltation filled my being ...
no negativity manifested ...
no anxiety surfaced ...
My husband's demeanor became very sweet.
Potential arguments melted away
and peacefully we went to sleep.
The next morning ~
my husband proclaimed that this day marked
the end of his excessive drinking!
I was stunned by this announcement,
which he had never made before.
For one year not a drop he consumed.
A sporadic light inebriation would occur after that,
but as of now ~ five years later ~
his statement still holds true.

Inexplicable is His Grace ...
In His eagerness to draw us ever closer
He paves the way.
Earlier He had admonished me so severely
and His Demands for loving ONLY HIM
had seemed so unapproachable ...
My efforts to do so ~ had been so weak ...
Now in total disregard for the imperfection of my attempts
He had opened the Door ...
The mere detection of the slightest presence

of a pure intention ~ melts His ever-giving Heart,
and He rushes to take a hundred steps towards us,
if only we earnestly struggle to take but one !!
Never could I have envisioned of my own accord
the inner display of Devotion ~
which allowed me to love Him
in such an effortless and exalted way,
that the desire for an outward change
simply ceased to arise.
Baffled by the powerful result
of this splendid moment of heartfelt devotion
I spent the remainder of the year
mostly contemplating this ever-expanding manifestation
of His Love and Grace ...
Whenever it would threaten to fade
I would hasten to find 'tricks' in order
to recapture its deeply inspiring glow
of Peace and Compassion.
I learned to call to mind
the memories of my Golden Days in His Presence.
Watching my hands ...
I would recall how they had experienced
the utter softness of His Lotus Feet ~
Listening to songs ...
I would remember the thrill
of hearing His Voice sing,
carrying me into His Divine Realm ~
Watching the movement of my feet ...
I relived the steps taken on His Holy Ground

approaching the Temple of all temples.
And so ...
my step was light during that year until ...
the golden memories became too hard to hold on to
and He once more called out to this helpless child
and wished for her to come ...

SIXTH VISIT

With contentment I looked back
at the yesterdays of that year
as I prepared for my next trip.
My companions would be my brother and my son.
The latter, by now ten years of age, had carefully saved
his hard earned money as a paperboy in order to satisfy
his intense longing to see the Lord ...
Brindavan was to be the place
where He graced us with this Sight Divine.
Day after day we were seated under the sacred Banyan Tree
enjoying fully the feast of Darshan.
Remembering how fruitful my efforts had been
in recapturing the moments spent in His Glorious Presence,
I drank ever deeper, with greater fervor
of this blissful NOW ...
storing high the Treasures Divine
for days of lesser Food ...
During this joyful occupation,
my Lord, one day, walked straight towards me
and expressed His Approval
by gently motioning me to take padnamaskar
while He repeatedly said, "*very happy, very happy...*"
Once again I was allowed to experience
the thrill of the touch of His Golden Lotus Feet!

Meanwhile I started to detect
an obvious obstruction on my path.

Rather subtly, but perseveringly steady,
the awareness of possible progress on my spiritual path
threatened to divert my attention
from the all-encompassing focus on ~ the Lord ~
to the dangerous pitfalls of self-interest.
Even though it might wear the mask
of aspiring for higher ideals ...
still the desire for personal inner growth
invokes an unhealthy fascination
which can easily sprout into an obsession ~
obscuring the original noble call
to awaken in Love Divine.
It becomes like the rotten core
bringing decay to the whole fruit.
Thoroughly afraid of the pangs of this poison
it became perfectly clear to me
that only true humility would grant me entrance
into His Land of Absolute Love.
Forever incapable of 'acquiring' humility
I knew of no other way than
uttering my plea for this sanctified trait
whenever the Lord entered my vision.
Over and over again I silently prayed,
"O Lord, shower me with true humility ..."
as He gracefully walked by me.
And ...
the sound of the rustling of His brilliant Robe
seemed to carry the echo of my words
as if responding to my quest

letting me know that I was heard
and that in due time the fruition would surface ...
Thus I spent my days ...
in silent prayer
deep gratitude
and eager absorption of the Light Divine
manifested fully in the human incarnation
of our Lord Supreme ...
O ~ what wonder ~ to be invited to witness
the Sublime Mystery of the Avatar,
the Lord of all Gods,
the very Embodiment of Being, Awareness and Bliss ...
Too deep to penetrate
too vast to fathom
too wondrous to let go
.. so inexplicably healing!
Suddenly the anticipated long road before us shrinks ...
The imagined hurdles on our spiritual path
fall away in the Light of His Love.
Dissolved are the struggles
as we fall in love with Love Supreme.
Somewhat astonished I started to sense
that the discovery of His Divine Incarnation
does not portray the start of the search for Light
but rather heralds the victory
over the Land of Shadows.
It brings into view the 'finish-line'.
O ~ how many lifetimes must we have spent
in ceaseless seeking and anguished prayers

.. .And now suddenly ...
the culmination of all our efforts in one feast,
the blissful Divine Sight of the Eternal One.
Unexpectedly ~ we are nearing the summit.
It is only the obstinate mind ~
so reluctant in accepting this supreme fact ...
so reluctant in giving up its self-made limits ...
always fighting in revolt ...
afraid of losing its precious life ...
.. but, dear mind, you go about in vain ~
you, too, shall perish in the blaze of His Fire...!
These contemplations made for an exquisite conclusion
of our stay; filled to overflowing was our cup
when Time reminded us to return to the Western World.

It was only a few weeks later
when Humility made her appearance
in a most unexpected manner.
Unannounced I received inwardly the following picture:
" .. alongside a beautiful sparkling river
at the foot of some high mountains,
there lived four sannyasis
linked together by their intense love for God.
Their spiritual brotherhood was deep-felt ~
A warm, genuine friendship surrounded them.
The youngest one of these four, however,
still showed signs of spiritual arrogance:
proud of his mode of living ...
appalled by the manifestation of the world ...

with self-righteousness luring him to believe
that renouncing the world paved the only way to purity.
His longing for God was sincere
but the immaturity of his insights
prevented him from embracing all manifestations,
thus blocking his pathway to the Immortal One.
His three companions were filled with
compassion for their brother ~
They agreed that in a future lifetime
they would gather again and create such a plot
that would force him to remain in the world
and face the challenge of going through it
instead of his continuous efforts, during many a lifetime,
of going around it.
This, however, would entail that one of them
had to take upon himself a most unwelcome role,
which meant that he voluntarily would give up
the greater portion of his awareness of God's Wisdom
during that lifetime ...!
The oldest one of these brothers
offered himself for this sacrifice ...
solely out of love for the struggling young one.
The two other ones would come along
to soften the blows he would have to deal with
and guide him to a greater purity of Love for God ...
And now ...
the older wiser one wears the disguise
of the earth-bound man ...
who is ever on the alert to carve away

any conventionality in modes of living
and hypocrisy in attitude in the one by his side,
his former arrogant brother,
who is now clothed in a female frame
capable of childbirth and consequently bound
by the ties of motherhood,
performing her inescapable duty.
The two remaining brothers
now live by her side as her daughter and son ..."

The picture was complete ...
Every disdaining thought about my husband's worldliness
now had to make a crushing fall!
The slightest entertainment of spiritual superiority
on my part ~ now reddened my face ...
as I suddenly became aware of
the depth of his sacrifice ...
the profound Love and Compassion...
born out of his vast fountain of Wisdom.
How clear his vision must be
since he voluntarily took upon himself the role of a blind man!
How wrong I had been ... all those years!
How humbling was the impact of this realization ...
How ridiculous that I had imagined
playing the role of the devout one ...
thereby fancying of being able
to turn my husband's eye to the inner world ...
O ~the arrogance of the petty mind!!
What fabulous wonder that I was allowed

to glimpse into this minute plot, one of the millions of His inscrutable
Master Plots.
The very core of my being stood still ...
in utter amazement I watched the disappearance
of the long nurtured opinion about our relationship.
Unspeakable love and reverence
towards my family members enveloped me.
Resentment and bitterness over the endured hardships
now took on the soft glow of understanding ...
.. suddenly the glorious link of brotherly love
was once again touched upon.
Clearly ~ the sharing of deep-felt devotion for God
was our only basis for togetherness.
All else vanished in its fold ...
A serene love blossomed forth from my heart.
Now simple laughter and innocent joy flowed
more easily through our household ~
as the memory of our longstanding friendship
became more vivid.
I was made to understand that my 'wise' husband
was not to remember those facts until a later date ~
his role was not yet finished, although steadily less harsh
as I would learn better and quicker over the years.
When his schooling for me will be completed
he shall remember fully the purpose for this lifetime
and instantly he shall leave his body
and once again be united with the Lord ...
The memory of the words spoken by my Lord,
during my interview, "*He is a very good man,*

a wonderful husband ..." now came back to me !
I recognized the infallible truthfulness of His statement
and ... mentally I bowed in reverence before
my 'saintly' husband.

Time, during this particular year,
allowed me a taste of 'timelessness'.
With the re-enforced ingredient of gratitude
and a deeper sense of humility
I encountered from time to time
.. the evaporation of the limits that mark 'Time'
.. the unnecessary build-up of its frame
.. the viewing of the experience of one moment
   unique in its manifestation
   naked in its aspect
   untouched by labels prefabricated by the mind
    and free from the anticipated consequence.
Such freedom arose from this blank slate ...
How utterly joyful became this moment ~
not perceived as a fragment in a pattern
but as a single, individual happening ~
not asking to be liked or disliked ...
and with this superb simplicity of being present
the Dance of Eternity captured my soul.

Like sweet surprises my Lord would often brighten
my days with these unexpected treasures.
Smilingly watching me ...
cherishing my delight,

as He would hand out yet another Gift
meanwhile beckoning me to hurry and
bathe again in His Concrete Presence,
for always ~ there is more to come ...

SEVENTH VISIT

Many, many years ago I had a dream,
the meaning of which was unclear to me at the time.
It went as follows:
" .. *On a grassy field upon a hill I was given two choices.*
I could use either a rope-ladder to climb up into
the infinite blue sky ~ this thought terrified me greatly,
as I am quite afraid of heights ~
or I could squeeze myself into a very small lift
which someone would push upwards.
But ~ in order to make use of the lift
I was to hold a very big book against my heart.
I choose to undertake the journey by lift.
Clenching the book to my chest I wriggled
into the open lift,
I was given an enormous push and up I went ...
Looking down on earth, I was at first scared
but suddenly there appeared two shining heavenly beings
right in front of me moving at the same speed.
Their radiance was so captivating
that fear left me instantaneously,
and in wondrous awe I gazed at them.
Now I could look all around me and feel overjoyed ...
the world slowly vanished ..."
After my wonderful experience
of reading the Holy Bhagavata,
I realized that this Sacred Scripture
was the Book Which I was told

to hold close to my heart ...
Indeed ~ it has made soar my thirsting soul
and as in the dream ...
the former perception of the world
is slowly being transformed.
This Holy Book with its endless accounts
of the Glories of our Lord truly deepens
ever more my love for Him ...
It is just like ~ at the beginning
of the blossoming of a new love ...
how ~ when one is attracted to another,
but still unfamiliar with his personality,
his doings and habits ~ one listens in rapt attention
to the tales about his character ...
How elated one becomes at the discovery
of his flawless nature ...
and the mind, heart and soul simply get
overwhelmed by love.
In precisely the same effortless manner
the reading about His Glory draws my attention
ever closer to the immense expanse of His Love.
Daily I read several pages and finish both volumes
within a year between my visits to the Holy Land of India,
to the Golden Lotus Feet of my Beloved Lord.

And so ... I decided to once again
dive fully into the nectar-like ocean
of the Holy Bhagavata during my oncoming visit.
In seven days, coinciding with the Dasara Festival,

I planned to complete this undertaking.
Thoroughly thrilled by this anticipation
I looked very much forward to this pilgrimage.
Aware of my inability to gauge
the proper depth of the auspiciousness
of the coming event ~ I called out to the ones I call
my saintly friends, to accompany me.
Oftentimes I read about their envy
of the contemporaries of the Avatar.
And therefore in all playfulness
I mentally gather around me those Great Ones
who know the Sacred Secret of these depthless moments ~
so, as not to waste a single drop of it
during the many instances that
the Divine Glory escapes my feeble mind.
Such joy I feel in my communications
with my Holy Friends!
With my 'invisible entourage of Friends'
I find myself in the taxi in Bangalore
and muse over the special time to come ...
I recall how the precious memories of my visits
have sustained my worldly life on the western hemisphere.
How wonderful that once again
He has called me to fill my cup anew.
As I open my eyes I read in astonishment
the words on a big billboard,
" .. Golden Memories!
     Refresh yourself with newly prepared memories! ..."
I can hardly believe my eyes

as I read the accurate expression
of the happy thoughts dancing on my mind.
Such sweet acknowledgement from my omnipresent Lord,
.. always letting me know
that He is the Eternal Witness of all my joys and sorrows.
Nearing my beloved ashram, my heart can hardly wait ...
Upon arrival I quickly adjust to its familiar routine
and after a few days
I am eager to start my seven-day reading.
This time the Dasara Festival is not celebrated
with the full complement of Brahmin Priests
and the Sacred Fire.
However ~ most every evening of this ten-day celebration
we receive the Blessing of His Spoken Word
and the supreme thrill of hearing
His Voice bring forth the Melody Divine ...
At the conclusion of the day
the Temple priest chants for about one hour
and about half the temple is allowed to be filled with people.
Every evening I hurry to the back porch
of my Lord's Temple, open the Bhagavata,
soak in Its Holy Words ...
and meanwhile wait patiently to enter His Abode.
Exactly during these seven days of reading
was I permitted to immerse myself
in the sacred vibrations of these powerful chants
in the very Temple of my Lord ~
to conclude each day of intense reading
in a grand manner!

This time, my sadhana of reading ~
which in no way means hardship to me,
but on the contrary, constitutes my greatest joy ~
brought forth a keen state of concentration.
Each time devotion swelled up in beautiful waves ...
my Lord urged me not to stop and dwell
but to go beyond this feeling of elation
and catch the upward motion of concentration.
This heightened energy often made
the crown of my head sore ~
as it seemed to pierce through the dull matter of my mind.
The sheer auspiciousness of these moments
permeated my being and I became aware
that the absence of this sanctified awareness
makes the conscious effort of remembrance
of the Lord a necessity.
With the aid of Golden Memories
we scrape clean the vessels of our senses
.. but with the perpetual awareness
of supreme auspiciousness
the senses fail to have a bottom
and the Flow of honeyed Oil of His Love Divine
knows no interruption.
The taste of this discovery made my heart
yearn a thousandfold ...
One blessed day as I was engaged in my reading,
during the interval of morning darshan and bhajans,
the Lord came outside and walked among
the men gathered in front of the Temple.

Suddenly He directed His Steps in my direction ~
from afar He walked in a straight line ...
This, He knows, is the most treasured sight
I wish to behold ...
.. for what could possibly overshadow
the experience of watching the Supreme Lord
walk towards me ...?
Drinking in deeply this inconceivable Grace
I became breathless ...
as He ~ at a short distance from me ~ turned to the right.
Painfully aware that I was incapable
of holding on to the holy sense of
this auspicious moment and saddened that it,
like the others, would be filed away
under my Golden Memories ...
my heart burst forth into the following prayer,
" .. O Lord of Unfathomable Glory,
    tell me, how can I capture a Gift of Eternity
    in a vessel with a bottom ...?
    Therefore, my Lord, if You long for me
    to keep Your Divine Gift, I pray ...
    make my senses bottomless,
    so Your Eternal nectarine Flow
    can stream unceasingly ..."
This prayer became my companion ~
expressing my intense yearning
to partake of His Supreme Love without a halt.
On the ninth day of Dasara
I concluded my week of reading.

The Glorious Victory Day arrived ...
Having a wonderful seat,
I spent a most blissful morning,
.. with beautiful songs emanating
from the voices of the college boys and girls,
and our Lord gracing us with His Splendorous Sight
and showering us with prasad.
After the gathering dispersed
a dear friend of mine and I lingered on ~
unable to pull ourselves away
from these Divine vibrations still filling the air.
With great joy we talked about the wondrous morning.
Our awe for His Miracle kept us engaged
in such a happy conversation for hours.
Suddenly His red Mercedes came around the corner ~
No one else was to be seen.
Quickly we ran to the drive-way.
Such good fortune !
After having bathed in His unique Grace
during the early hours, and intensified its glow
by our expounding on His Mystery of Love ...
we now, once again, beheld our Lord..!
Overwhelmed by His infinite Love
I sank to my knees alongside the car.
He bestowed upon me the sweetest of all smiles
and raised His Hand in the gesture of blessing ...
As I watched the car turn around the corner,
wonderful words started to emerge from within.
Tears welled up in my eyes

as I hastily got up and through a blurry vision
walked quickly to my room.
I grabbed pen and paper and wrote down the words
that seemed to flow into my consciousness.
I cried when I finished this first 'poem'.
Somehow ~ the words expressed so accurately
the joys of my soul ...
Never before had I been able to create so effortlessly.

Soon it was time to leave.
A sense of wonderful fulfillment filled my being.
Once the long plane travel had begun
a sudden outpour of words became unstoppable ...
Poem after poem emerged ~
mesmerized by this process
I was unable to feel fatigue and
was totally incapable of sleep.
As soon as I would put down my head
a new flow of Melody arrived.
Just when I thought that I was running out of paper,
the stewardess handed me the free gift,
a pen and writing paper ~
not just one she gave me, but three of each ...!
Flabbergasted by this new manifestation
of His Love and Grace, I asked my Lord
what He wished me to do with these writings.
Immediately He responded ...
With amazing clarity He urged me to write down
the words handed to me, collect the poems and

bring them to Him on my next visit.
Right then He gave me the title for the collection,
"Sprinkles of Golden Dust"...
and showed me in a flash the design of the cover.
With this new field of creativity
ever beckoning me to enter upon it
I arrived home.
Difficult it was ...
to function in my role as mother and wife,
to perform the duties expected from me ...
since more often than not
the surge of words kept me spellbound
and the desire to submerge myself
in its Wave of Bliss became so irresistible.
Former insights and revelations re-surfaced
now clothed in melodious words,
expressing the essence of my experiences.
Forever humbling was this new occupation ...
Crystal clear ~ it showed my inability
to compose such words of inspiration
of my own accord ...
for at times,
most unexpectedly, while being engaged
in worldly activities with the mind preoccupied
with secular thoughts ~ He stopped me,
urged me to find pen and paper
and write ...
phrases of such eloquence
which my mind, so meager,

could never produce ~
But the Royal Resplendent Resident of my heart, ever so eager,
brought forth this lordly Melody
with effortless ease ...!
How incredible is the expression of His immense Love ...!
Repeatedly my senses were unable
to cling to a personal view as He exposed
the core of the matter perceived and
made stream a touch of the Sacred Flow of His Truth
throughout my being ...
and raised my awareness again and again
to the exalted Silence of Auspiciousness.
Now I realized ...
He had answered my prayer !
My quest for 'bottomless senses'
in order to receive His unceasing Nectar
had come true ...
beyond all imagination!!
As the months passed by
He taught me how to live
with this Fountain of sweet Gold ~
It became easier to restrain myself
and not to feel frustrated when the opportunity
for delving into 'writing' was not there ...,
to grow in faith, that the words would not disappear
but simply re-enter at the proper time.
His Commands became more precise
as time went on ...
demanding ever more concentration.

Now He would not just overpour me with words
but gave several topics at once,
often opposing one another, to expound upon.
Rather than flow away in melting emotions
I was to dive into the very essence
of the subject handed to me ~
very still I allowed myself to reach out
to its depthless origin ...
There He showed me, to the extent possible
for my immature soul, in wordless communication
its wondrous meaning ...
Then ~ as I left this sacred stillness
the words began to flow unhindered
on the blank sheet of paper
resting on my lap.

And so we danced
through a much Bliss-filled year
leaving my soul in the vast rapture of awe
for the continuous unfolding
of the Sublime Mystery of His Love Divine.

EIGHTH VISIT

After writing down 108 poems
I busied myself with the design
of a blue velvet cover with a golden lining
and the embroidered outline of a lotus on the front.
This would become the ornamental cloth
with which I covered the collection of poems
in order to present it to Him with the utmost care ...
Protected by my array of saris
it was to make a safe trip in my suitcase across the oceans.
My daughter, almost sixteen at the time,
joined me on this year's journey.
As we were preparing to depart from the airport
I hastily bought a postcard and sent it to a friend.
It was an exquisite picture of two swans flying into the sunset.
Playfully I wrote:
" .. and off we go ...
    the Flight of the Swans into the Lord's Sunset ..."
And with this sense of awe
we took off into the already darkening sky.
Our stop-over was in Malaysia.
During the evening we spent there
I wrote down the following words,
".. The Lord has called me once again
    and quickly I hasten to His Sight.
    Suddenly worldly affairs seem to have dropped away
    and the road is made clear ...
    In great wonder and amazement

I watch the unfolding of this event.
I find it inexplicable that this is His Will for me
and I can't help wondering
what gifts He has in store for me this time.
I try not to block His Divine Flow of Grace
by dreaming up selfish prayers,
for I want to enable Him to enjoy freely
the outpouring of the planned gifts for me ...
He is like the mother who in great joy
secretly prepares a festivity for her child ~
busily decorating and wrapping the presents
meanwhile happily anticipating the joy
she will bring to her child.
And so ~ this child is being ushered
to the place of festivities ...
but she is not yet allowed to peek
behind the curtains or look at
the wrapped boxes with ribbons!
Over the years I have learned to succumb
to His Plot and willingly I play my part ...
Today my part expects me to play the waiting game
and gently I allow the mist of travelling details
with its tiring schedules to envelop me ..."
Little did I know that He would take
this comparison so seriously...!
The next day I found, to my great surprise,
the grounds of Brindavan richly decorated.
And at the time of our arrival,
festivities were going on ~ on stage,

and I discovered my Lord seated
in the audience enjoying the show.
It turned out to be the Onam Festival!
My joy knew no boundaries.
Soon after the musical show had finished
He got up and ordered prasad to be distributed.
And so ... within one hour from when I landed in Bangalore
He gave me His Darshan surrounded
by a festive atmosphere and fed my fatigued body
with His Blessed Food ...
I knew that once again,
I had been drawn into His Ocean of Love
and all that I had to do was to watch and witness
as He so thoroughly enjoys
the granting of unexpected gifts ...
That evening my great good fortune
was enriched a thousandfold,
since He decided to welcome me
with a wonderful discourse followed by a Song Divine.
Supremely satisfied by this most festive first day
I laid my tired body to rest for the night.
It was not until the next day
that I became more acutely aware of the absence
of the Holy Banyan Tree.
For a short time I felt the pangs of pain
of not beholding that Sacred Spot
where I had received such Grace.
But not for long did He allow me to be sentimental ...,
for immediately I was drawn into

that magnificent magnetic field of Divine Energy
present in the Sai Ramesh Hall.
Not used to the daily routine of this new hall
I was most pleasantly surprised
by hearing the college boys sing bhajans
in the afternoon during the Lord's Darshan.
Immediately it transported me
to His boundless Land of Bliss.
As the songs continued to fill the air
the Lord, seated on the stage,
kept piercing His Eyes into my being ...
and suddenly I felt powerful energy
penetrating my spine and head ...
I needed great concentration to remain upright.
With this unexpected surge of Light
came an intense profound longing
for full awareness of Absolute Reality.
O ~ how I yearned for the Door to Pure Knowledge
to be opened ... and I begged Him to do so.!
Bhajans came to an end, as He got up to leave.
The door to His Garden opened, and as He walked through it ~
I saw two swans fly up into the orange-colored sky ...
and I remembered the postcard I had sent to my friend,
" .. the Flight of the Swans
    into the Lord's Sunset ..."!
Tears of longing
tears of joy
tears of gratitude flowed freely at this moment!
That evening I truly stumbled through

the village on our way to our room.
My spine and head were still in sweet pain
from the sudden Flood of Light
and my daughter had to literally support me
since I kept falling into walls ...
All through that night I was aware of this sensation
and quietly I tried to hold on ...
The following day I carried with me
the manuscript wrapped in royal blue velvet.
Now that I had finished this collection
and had brought it to Him ~
I felt content having done what He had told me to do.
My next question was,
did He wish for me to share these writings with others ...?
If so, I prayed that He would let me know beyond a doubt
that all the words I had heard and written down
were correct ..., that no falsehood had been uttered ...
I asked Him to give me a concrete sign
of His Approval and promised that if He did not find
these writings worthy of approval I would discard them
into the wastebasket.
Almost at the end of the hall were we seated,
on the inside of the aisle, when the Lord made His entrance.
Perfectly relaxed I watched the loving scene
of His tender caring for His flock.
Since we were so far back
I did not at all anticipate any outward attention.
As He came nearer and nearer
I realized that my presumption could be wrong ...

My heart started to beat faster.
Suddenly He was right there ...
I lifted up the manuscript
as He reached out and took letters
from all around us, meanwhile fixing His Eyes
upon my collection,
.. but He kept going and went on to the men's side.
At that point I felt that, clearly,
He had taken notice of the contents,
but had not reacted and I was willing
to do away with it.
Then ... He turned around and came
straight towards me without taking His Eyes
off the manuscript.
Again I lifted it up and as soon as
He stopped in front of me He started to make
vibhuthi and poured this 'Divine Dust'
into my hand and my daughter's.
Some of it fell upon my collection
which He had titled Sprinkles of Golden Dust ...!
What perfect concrete proof of His Approval ...!
No words were spoken,
no further outer communication was necessary!
As He turned to walk away
a great peace came over me.
Now the project of the poems had been fully completed,
I could put it to rest ...
With silent persistence He seemed to call on me
to be alert ...

to stay open ...
as the gradual unfolding of His Glory
would ever more demand a greater Emptiness.
Each time during the moments
of intense communication, especially
those power-filled afternoon Darshans
accompanied by bhajans,
He emphasized this point over and over again.
Look ONLY at Me ...
Speak ONLY to Me ...
Long ONLY for Me ...
Do not busy yourself with the world's busyness ...
Your one-pointed focus will ever more swallow up
the unnecessary 'necessities' of life.
With the amazing touch of gentle firmness
He led me to a seemingly ever-widening Silence.
.. Silence ~ the Foundation of His Mansion of Glory ...
"*Rest in this Stillness, My child*
and I shall reveal to you
the Secrets of My Being ...
Effortlessly you shall roam
on the Pastures of Perfect Peace
and joyously play in My Land of Love Divine."
He allowed me to somehow maintain
this heightened sense of silence
for periods at a time during this stay ~
introducing me to a deeper taste of His Reality,
always inducing a more ardent longing
for His unfathomable Truth ~

thereby sharpening my alertness,
preparing my nerve-system for
the onslaught of His omnipotent Light.

His urgent prompting for one-pointed attention
on my part, led me to reach for the booklet
with the Thousand Names of Vishnu.
As it had been my practice to read
these Thousand Names each time I had finished
the Holy Bhagavata ~ I had acquired
a great fondness for this Rosary of
His immaculate Attributes.
Now ~ while waiting for each Darshan ~
I started to read these.
After a few Darshans I began to notice
that each time, as soon as I finished reading
the last Name, the Lord ~ Vishnu Himself ~
made His Entrance ...!
This went on for the rest of my visit.
This response strengthened my conviction
of the immediate effectiveness of this practice.
Our last afternoon bhajan session arrived.
Like the previous glorious gatherings,
this one ~ but more intensely so ~ elevated
my soul to a Field of motionless Absoluteness.
His almost constant Gaze from His Seat seemed
to burn all hindering obstacles
and carried me swiftly and relentlessly
to a Truth ~ thus far unperceived by me.

Completely spellbound ... with acute alertness
I partook of this Nectar Divine
Which He so abundantly poured
into this starving being.
He became surrounded by Light to my outer eye.
The whole stage had turned into an Ocean of Light
with the Lord of All Radiance seated in the middle.
Never before was I so engulfed
in the awareness of sitting
at the Feet of the Almighty God ...
Bhajans went on for longer than usual and
I realized that this was His farewell "inner interview" for me.
My eyes remained fixed upon His Form as He left ...
I gently closed my eyes
and the Sea of Grace kept me aloft.
Ever so strong and persistent
did the thought re-enter my mind,
that this moment marked the end of my 'outer' life
and announced the beginning of my 'inner' life.
I looked up ...
no longer did the stage appear the same,
suddenly it no longer felt like the Temple of my Lord ...
and then ... His Words came,
" .. *That is right!*
   My glorious Temple of Light
   with My Form seated on the Throne
   as you have just perceived it ~
   is now in you ...!"

Upon returning home I indulged in the marvelous sunsets
on the wide beaches of California.
Every evening the bright orange setting sun
over the vast expanse of the magnificent waters
of the Pacific called me to experience its wonder
and drew me ever more inward ...
With beautiful ease it became His Temple of Light
with my Lord clad in orange ...
O ~ how I cherished these evening-meditations.
My ever-growing Love for His inconceivable Divinity
compelled me once more to search
for expressions to express the Inexpressible.
During the time that I had read
the Thousand Names of Vishnu ~
I had often longed for a few more words after each Name,
not just an explanation, but rather an extended emphasis
of Its grandeur ..., so one could linger a little longer
on each sublime meaning.
Now I decided to delve into this impossible task myself
and see if it was His prompting that gave me this longing ...
As soon as I picked up my pen
and focussed on each Name and mused
over the given explanation ~
the longed-for prolongation presented itself.
These words took me again and again
to the place where I had no choice
but to look ONLY at Him.
This constant dwelling on His unending Attributes
made for the perfect practice of

concentration and alertness ~
the very lesson which He had so intensely
imprinted on my soul.
With great joy I busied myself daily
with the writing of the "Thousand Songs of Lord Vishnu".

Great was my surprise when, one evening,
during my sunset meditation,
my Lord told me that my days in California
were coming to an end ...
I was shocked about this sudden revelation.
No outer signs that would indicate an oncoming change
were to be found ...
and I was so happy where I was at ...!
With a confused and somewhat unwilling mind
I tried to listen ... as His Presence told me that:
.. a new phase in my life had begun
.. the sense of endless expanse, which I so much felt
   on these beaches, was only a foretaste for the time to come
.. it was time to move on and distance myself from those
   whom I had known for so many years
.. no ties were to bind me,
   although wonderful relationships were present ~
   by which I had greatly benefitted ~
   it was time to break through them
   and let no one's thought-waves touch my quest
   for an ever intenser, more pronounced inner life.
.. at a much later date I might return to California
   but by then much will have changed ~

not necessarily in the shape of its physical landscape ~
but in the existing make-up of my thoughts and emotions,
since this will be thoroughly altered by then.
With this unexpected information,
which I shared with the children,
I awaited the avalanche of events.
One simple phone-call, a few weeks later,
set the move into motion.
Seemingly unconquerable difficulties
with a business relation of my husband
made it obvious that his business would no longer
continue in the same manner.
Without his awareness of the premonition given to me,
my husband immediately suggested that maybe
we should relocate in a less expensive area and start anew
with the small savings we had accumulated.
After an initial sadness of leaving
our California beach life
the charm of a new adventure soon started
to inspire the whole family.
The preparations took place with amazing speed.
Every excess piece of furniture was sold.
Only the minimum required ~ we decided to pack.
With the map of the USA in front of us
we tried to decide upon a destination.
For no particular reason at all,
somehow the state of Virginia appealed to us most.
The journey across this mighty land
was extremely joyful ~

how incomparable was my state of mind
with the early days of traveling
under uncertain circumstances.
Now ~ I treasured the utter freedom
of no place, no ties, no specific plans
.. for I felt the absolute certainty of His Guidance,
which brought forth the sweet simplicity
of unconditional 'being' ...
Unaware of the fact that, the first night in Virginia,
we actually landed in our future place of settlement ~
we still explored other regions
of this state for one more week.
Unmistakably we kept being called back
to that high mountain range ...
We found a lovely dwelling on top
of the mountain with a spectacular view
of a beautiful valley.
With the National Forest at our back door
I soon found myself exploring its many hiking trails.
These majestic mountains, at this time
covered with the magic touch of snow ~
interspersed with breathtaking vistas ~
generated a deep sense of
Holy Silence and Glorious Solitude within me.
Indeed, the elation I had felt at the beach,
now seemed to propel itself into a steadier,
more 'grounded' awareness of His infinite Vastness.
The forest became my shrine.
Daily I walked into the woods behind the house

and made one of the big rocks my seat for meditation.
There, my 'meetings' with my Lord
became astonishingly tangible ...
our 'conversations' clearer ...
His explanations easier to grasp ...
It was here that He wished for me
to understand the meaning of Dharma
as I should see it and practice it.

" .. *Dharma, My dear child, has to embrace*
the whole scope of thoughts, words and deeds.
In all these ~ there is one underlying rule:
NEVER draw attention to yourself
but instead ... pay attention to ME ...!
In your WORDS ~ be clear
do not be hesitant
speak with confidence
do not carry the veil of shyness,
for it displays pre-occupation
with self-importance and thereby
unveils your vanity
do not express cleverness for it
does not enhance My Presence!
In Your ACTIONS ~ be precise
do not waver
allow yourself to rely upon the
certainty of My Authority and
relinquish the thought of doership
In your THOUGHTS ~ only entertain the thought of
your bond with Me

*Your mind is still crowded with the
various games of relativity, therefore
use its natural tendency and
strengthen your relationship with ME
Call ceaselessly upon My Presence
in all matters*
*The attentive application of this 'inner' Dharma
brings forth an honest simplicity,
which spills over into the effortless expression
of 'outer' Dharma.
You see, My dear, the Source of true Dharma
is foremost an intense Love for Me...
it touches the inner fields of your being,
it purifies your words, thoughts and deeds
and each of them will become
a Testimony of My Holy Presence ...
the very Manifestation of My Silent Glory ...
You will live in Loving Truth
            displaying Truthful Love ..."*

NINTH VISIT

Now the job of cleaning house was no longer there
to support so reassuringly my annual trips to India.
I would sometimes wonder
how I would so quickly amass sufficient money
to undertake my most precious pilgrimage,
in order not to skip a year ~ which posed
an unbearable thought to me.
I did not have to wait long for an answer.
My brother told me that from now on
our stepmother had decided to give annually,
to each of her stepchildren, the generous amount of $600.
This would take care of half my ticket!
Once again ~ He had provided in a most unexpected way ...!
The other half was easily earned by working
in a small rest-home for the elderly.
My son's desire to accompany me
enabled him to find a job and work hard enough
to materialize the fulfillment of his longing
to be part of this year's pilgrimage.
My brother met with us in Bombay,
and before long the three of us arrived in Bangalore
and quickly settled in a hotel in Brindavan.

Time utterly lost its meaning ...
when ~ once again ~ I found my body
seating itself on that shiny floor of this Sacred Hall,
wrapped around by the graceful foldings of an elegant sari ...

100

And smiling I closed my eyes
as I watched the play of the intervening moments of one year
simply vanish from the screen of my mind.
Seated closely to the stage
I clearly caught His gentle Smile resting upon me ~
as He slowly moved His Hands upwards
the moment He entered the Hall.
Such contentment seemed to flow from Him ...
and such an invitation to merge into His Aura of Truth ...
I felt that not a minute was wasted,
no soothing or pampering seemed necessary
for my fatigued body ...
no gently adjusting to these austere surroundings ...
.. but immediately He seemed to demand
that I was to be thrown into His Fire.
Stop wasting time with thinking ~
enter without questions
with relentless courage.!
As much as possible I tried to obey these demanding commands.
The following day He playfully took possession
of my notion of doership and I clearly felt
His perceiving of 'my' thoughts and emotions,
His enjoying of 'my' functions as a being,
His immediate Companionship ...
.. He simply had taken over, and this state brought forth
an unspeakable sweetness within my heart.
It fastened with immeasurable strength the Cord of Love.
O, Lord, I wondered, is this a minute taste
of the Sublime Devotion of Radha ...?

Without this feeling ~ all is lost!
All withers away into nothingness ...
because the 'regular' perceiver is but the deceiver,
who creates illusions and holds fast onto
its phantom structures, thereby strangling
the chance to experience the all-blissful Reality.
O ~ how clearly I could see that now!
The depth of these incredible moments
revealed the absoluteness of my Total Dependence
on the Lord and with this sharp realization
came the instant certainty of
His Constant Presence within me :
.. like the helpless child
   who does not survive without the mother...
   its urgent need for her presence ...
   its full dependence on her constant care
   demands her attendance to the infant at all times!!
This simple comparison ~
now suddenly flooded my soul with a spontaneous joy.
Nothing is possible without Him!
From those blissfully charged moments on
I could only pray that He would steal my mind
and transform my heart forever ...
During the following bhajan session
I again had a seat close to His Chair.
The soul-stirring music and songs
set the stage for a beautiful silent conversation
with my radiant Lord.
No sooner had I phrased my above-mentioned request
than the Lord turned to me and shook His Head ...
Quite taken aback by this instant unexpected response,

I tried to re-phrase my plea ...
but, alas, the same rejection occurred!
Again and again I asked in various ways
for the lifting up of my soul ...
and each time He immediately fixed His Gaze
upon me and shook His Head...
Finally His Eyes remained focussed on me
gently smiling ...
waiting patiently...
until I became still enough
to hear His Plea for me ..:
" .. *Stop the asking, My foolish child!*
   What I have to give you is greater
   than you could ever imagine.
   It is beyond any descriptions,
   it defies words, thought and dreams.
   Whatever you ask from Me is only
   a part of the state which I am drawing you into!
   No need to desire fragments
   when I am handing you the 'Whole' ...
   The merging into My Glory is far superior
   to any notion about Knowledge or Devotion
   that you might entertain ...,
   Allow Me to delight Myself greatly ...
   Do not block My Flow of Grace
   and make diminutive what I wish to be immeasurable ...
   Leave clear the Field of Thinking ~
   Be free even from lofty requests ...
   The natural unfolding of My Love is supremely grand.
   Do not hinder it by begging for 'heavenly crumbs'.
   I ask you: "let Grandeur be at its Grandest ...!"

Nothing remained to be related,
the Emptiness my infinite Lord had created within me
now left me Full ...

Our glorious days in Brindavan came to an abrupt end,
as we got word that the Lord would leave
for Puttaparthi the next day.
Hastily we prepared ...
After arriving in Puttaparthi we discovered
all the wonderful changes brought about
on and around the ashram-grounds.
Daily I went up to the Meditation Tree
where the pure vibrations of this Holy Spot
seemed to penetrate my soul and
embrace my being with a Golden Light.
So as not to lose these touches of Truth
I engaged myself in japa during
the long waiting hours before Darshan.
Such comfort I received from holding my japamala,
keeping it in the folds of my sari ~
my fingers would caress its beads with each silent repetition
of either the Holy Gayatri or His Blessed Name.
It brought me great joy to keep
this occupation out of sight of my fellow-pilgrims.
I discovered how it heightened my elation
when I kept secret these blissful communications.
O ~ my friend ~ keep still the tongue ...
forever more sacred will become your secret ...
ever more precious ...
ever more exalting ...

your eyes will speak of your rapture,
your aura will reveal the felicity of your heart,
no need for the spoken word!
Miraculously this practice banished
any notion of speculation
any hint of anticipation ...
In the presence of NOW
the waiting stopped ...
I simply forgot that sitting there implied 'waiting' ...!
The blankness of my mind made me
understand the fallacy of entertaining
expectations of any kind and how
its hypnotic power alone sets Time in motion ...
In the midst of this joy
my Lord appeared suddenly and walked
quickly by our row of ladies.
As He passed by He turned to me
and gave the brightest smile I had ever received!
O ~ how it deepened the awareness of Timelessness ...,
which I had just experienced.
A simple Glance from His Divine Eyes
sets fire to the sparkle of the smallest insight!

Skillfully He pulled me into His Ocean of Love
so all-embracing ...
so inebriating ...
.. Then ~ quite abruptly did the sweetness
of loving communication change into
a sharp felt pain of the still existing separation.
The deeper I felt 'connected'

the more I suddenly seemed to realize
the duality of our relationship.
Now ~ my whole being began to yearn
with great intensity for merging with Him.
As an uncontrollable wave this immense sadness
came over me ...
Tears were unstoppable ...
Any sense of 'me' or 'my personality'
brought me a nauseating disgust.
The inner-felt agony began to cause
actual physical pain throughout my body.
I could not bear the thought that once again
I would have to gather enough courage
to carry me through another year in worldly surroundings.
Enough ~ I had of courage to wear the mask
of an 'individual' ...
enough ~ I had of enjoying the challenge
of discovering wonderful connections
between the events of the secular world
and my devotion to the Lord ...
The sweet marvel of Love ~
that sublime connection between
the Beloved and the lover
had turned into a piercing pain of not being united.
No longer did the bond entice me.
My soul seemed to scream for the merging
into the Light of the Absolute.
Nothing appealed to me any longer ..
During the days to come this feeling intensified ...
and with great restraint I had to fight back

my tears ~ since they seemed to well up constantly.
No relief did my Lord bring me ~
The remaining Darshans were short
and only seemed to heighten my yearning.
The last night before our departure
I received a dream in which
the Lord appeared as Mother Kali.
After my full prostration before Her
She gave me Her Blessing and told me:
" .. *Everything will be alright ...* "
Reluctantly consoled I took leave
of my beloved Prasanthi Nilayam
and through a heavy mist of tears
we drove to Bangalore in order to start
our long journey 'homeward' bound.

The friendly rolling hills of Virginia
and the sweet disposition of my welcoming husband
somewhat lessened the sharp contrast
between the two continents, the two worlds.
It, however, gave me barely enough reason to breathe ...
As the daily routine of my household resumed
I felt as if dead to the world.
Everything had lost its meaning ...
for where there used to be sweet contentment
.. I now felt an inner senselessness.
The despair of darkness blackened my days ~
each morning I awoke with a feeling of heaviness
and time and again I had to somehow
keep myself from crying uncontrollably.

My Lord had disappeared completely
and I had no idea where to find Him ...
or how to remember His Love ...
Emptiness is all I found !
Finally after several weeks I woke up
one morning and felt a dim light
at the horizon of my mind ...
My heart fluttered with hope ~
could it be true that He would return...?
Gradually the Light emerged to the extent
that I felt alive once more ...!
Searching through the rubble of those devastating days
I realized that this process had flattened
my ground drastically ...
in order for a thorough renewal to take place.
A deeper touch had to emerge -
a more profound understanding was necessary.
This depthless abyss had taken from me
each and every idea thus far conceived about
spirituality with its broad spectrum of surrender,
devotion, the Goal of Self-realization ...
From this levelled ground
a new sense of 'yearning' took root ...
the kind of yearning that does not tolerate
the hypocrisy of likes and dislikes,
a yearning which absorbs all and
forgoes the pendulum of relative existence.
The soothing pain of this yearning
overshadows by far the raw sense of pleasure ...
It beckoned me to get so immersed

in this longing for merging with the Beloved
that I would get Lost in Love ...
timeless ... formless existence in Being ...
where the obsession of Becoming evaporates ...
The arrows, shot forth from this new awareness,
reached so deep into my soul
that it left me with the ultimate conclusion
that this pain is not possible ...!
The very pain that I experienced could not have any reality,
.. since the Lord loved me more than a thousand mothers
and therefore would be utterly incapable of inflicting
agony upon His own child...?
Out of His Love, so immeasurable,
He could not wish for me to be somewhere
where He is not ...
He only desires for me to be there
where I would find Him more fully ..!
Therefore all that seems to separate me from Him
is sheer illusion.
I had no choice but to dismiss their 'realities'
if I longed to truly understand
the Love of my Divine Mother ...
and approach Her unselfishly.
This revelation struck with lightning
through my mind and brought the non-existence
of our assumed realities to the surface -
not as a 'reasoned-out' conclusion
but as a radical acceptance filling my heart
with wonder ...
Sparkles of the Bright Sun of Non-Dualistic Awareness

fell upon my delighted being.
At this point my Lord innocently asked me
to relate to you, my dear friend, the events of my life -
but, in actuality, as I picked up my pen to do so,
He was the One Who told me
.. how the sequence had taken place
.. how and why the revelations had come to me
   at their time of exposure
.. how each and every step was perfect in its expression
   and full in purpose
.. how His early whisperings had drawn me
   out of the density of the so-called world
.. how sweet gratitude had made the soil fertile
   for a true Love for the Divine
.. how devotion had welled and ripened
   and draped everything with the Mantle of Awe
.. how the harshness of dualism had become less severe
.. how He had planted the seed
   and how it, irreversibly, shall grow
.. how this Seed of Pure Grace blossoms
   more speedily under the Sunshine of Contentment
   and when saturated with Showers of Blissful Devotion
.. and then - when my Love has expanded
   to such an extent that it can withstand
   the immensity of His Light -

                      all concepts shall collapse,
                      all motion shall recede into
                      the Stillness of the Absolute,
                      the Heart of His Being ...

With each new chapter He has held me spellbound
as I was eager to watch His explanations
for His 'doings' for me ...
And so ...
by asking me to write
I had to listen ...
as His Words revealed the Music of this 'Song'
in order for me to grasp more deeply, more acutely,
the unfailing Law, the instigator of events,
which brings us ultimately to the
                  Point of Radical Acceptance
                  of the Immediate Reality of HIS LOVE.

AND THE SONG CONTINUES ...

Supreme is His Glory
Boundless is His Love

The splendorous union of these two
brings forth His multitudes of 'Songs'.
Out of Love He sings ...
out of Glory He creates ...
Each Song unique in melody,
each incomparable to another.
Ever unfolding His incomprehensible Majesty,
infinitely revealing endless 'Songs'.

This Song, too, is without end ...
as He carries me higher and higher
into the deep blue skies of His Wonder
unveiling the mighty Magic of His Maya,
His innocent Play ...
His fabulous Sport ...
where He excels in the elusiveness of 'motion',
where He allows the notion of ignorance to occur.
In the very Stillness of His Thought of Motion
lies the Essence of Illusion.
It expresses the enticing invitation
to 'link' together the views of static images
and thereby produces the fascination of a 'tale' ...

The so-called 'motion' stirred up by relating
one thing to another suggests
the 'reality' of its conclusion
and Time is its enthusiastic corroborator.
And thus ...
infinite possibilities of multitudes of 'scenarios'
evolve endlessly from His playful Mind,
creating the utterly false idea
of beginnings and ends ...
His Display of this Divine Dance induces
the maddening obsession with 'becoming',
the phantom play of 'progress' -
and as helpless puppets we succumb to its steps,
carrying with us the unnecessary Burden of Guilt
which solidifies Yesterday ...
meanwhile entertaining hopeful Anticipations
which concretes Tomorrow ...
thereby leaving behind the unique Fragrance of Today ...
Lost in the sheer folly of Illusion
we prolong our self-proclaimed 'existence'
in our quest for 'perfection' -
thereby acknowledging the very structure
we wish to deny ...
And out of fear we create do's and don'ts
meanwhile emphasizing our doership, until our mental fatigue seeks
out the Heart ...
where the Mountain of spiritual self-interest
crumbles under the pure pressure
of His all-embracing Love ...

And finally we realize how the 'part'
has made absurd attempts to become perfect
while all the time the 'Whole' has been complete
and perfectly perfect ...
And how each 'part' of the 'Whole' has to have
the same characteristic, ... PERFECTION ...!

And so He sings ...
and I listen ...
drawing me ever closer
teaching me to hush ...
for His Words shall come ...
The sweet nectar He allows me to taste
while writing has gradually won me over
to do likewise in daily affairs -
to let go ...
to surrender ...
to watch the unravelling of Time ...
to accept the moments of 'imperfection' ...
the times of Shade ...
and find them miraculously folded
into His Master Plot.
Sublime is His Craftsmanship -
infinitely sweet His Care ...
And I discover
that He does not shower me
with these wondrous Gifts of Joy and Elation
for 'my' satisfaction -
but it is ONLY HIM enjoying

His own Glory through me ...!
O - how this discovery
silences any sense of ego
and propels the awareness of Austere Beauty ...
and how it ever deepens my yearning
to be more empty ...
so my Lord can uninterruptedly
and ever more unhindered exult
in the Majesty of His Creation
with ...
His Songs of Love and Wisdom
endlessly reverberating
through His Realm of the Absolute.

O - how incomprehensibly Blessed
are Today's Days ...
for supremely Auspicious is our human birth
during the Golden Advent of the Avatar.
The Poorna Avatar ...
The Ultimate Embodiment of Being
                                   Awareness
                                   Bliss ...
The Sublime Enchanter of the Heart ...
He is the One
Who does not merely point the Way
but out of His unfathomable Compassion
He lifts up His child
and carries her Home ...

the Magnitude of His Love
        annihilating all notions
the Expanse of His Glory
        stilling all murmurs ...
humbly we become willing participants
        in the VICTORY OF THE AVATAR.

J A I   S A I   R A M

EPILOGUE

.. if now, you find this story merely interesting
I have failed to convey to you
the Message He has given me, but ...
.. if instead, your heart is lifted high
and your soul rejoices with supreme gladness
over the wondrous workings of His Majesty,
I have succeeded in the task He has handed me.
For He desires for you to know
that you, as you are, are His Song
.. the EXPRESSION OF HIS JOY
.. the MANIFESTATION OF HIS GLORY
.. the VERY EMBODIMENT OF HIS LOVE

GLOSSARY

Ashram - a community dedicated to spiritual life

Atma - name for the inexpressible Absolute

Avatar - a divine incarnation

Bhagavan - a term most appropriate for the glory of the Lord

Bhajans - devotional songs

Darshan - the sight of a holy man

Dasara - ten day Hindu festival

Deepavali - festival of Lights, celebrating victory of light over darkness

Dharma - righteous conduct

Gayatri - a most sacred ancient prayer

Japa - the repetition of a prayer

Maya - the veil of illusion covering the light of truth

Onam - a Hindu festival

Padnamaskar - the homage of prostration at the feet of a holy man

Prasanthi Nilayam - Abode of Heavenly Peace, name of Sai Baba's ashram

Prasad - food blessed by a holy man

Poorna Avatar - full embodiment of the divine

Sadhana - practice of spiritual discipline

Sari - the garment worn by women in India

Sannyasi - one who out of love for God renounces everything

Vibhutti - sacred ash materialised by Sai Baba